THE BAFFLED PARENT'S
GUIDE TO
COACHING
TEE BALL

Bing Broido

Cofounder and President, T•BALL USA Association

Ragged Mountain Press / McGraw-Hill

Camden, Maine • New York • Chicago • San Francisco
Lisbon • London • Madrid • Mexico City • Milan • New Delhi
San Juan • Seoul • Singapore • Sydney • Toronto

Dedicated to Alana, Jack, and Anika, and their generation,
and to Lois Richards, cofounder of the T•BALL USA Association—
my personal coach.

The McGraw·Hill Companies

1 2 3 4 5 6 7 8 9 0 DOC DOC 0 9 8 7 6 5 4 3

Copyright © 2003 by Ragged Mountain Press

Library of Congress Cataloging-in-Publication Data
Broido, Bing, [date]–
  The baffled parent's guide to coaching tee ball / Bing Broido.
       p.   cm.—(The baffled parent's guides)
Includes index.
  ISBN 0-07-138738-2
  1. T-ball. 2. Baseball for children—Coaching. I. Title. II. Series.

GV881.5 .B73 2003
  796.357′8—dc21   2002012970

Questions regarding the content of this book should be addressed to
Ragged Mountain Press
P.O. Box 220
Camden, ME 04843
www.raggedmountainpress.com

Questions regarding the ordering of this book should be addressed to
The McGraw-Hill Companies
Customer Service Department
P.O. Box 547
Blacklick, OH 43004
Retail customers: 1-800-262-4729
Bookstores: 1-800-722-4726

Photographs by Gene Sowell unless otherwise noted.
Illustrations by Christopher Dowling.

Contents

Part One
Coaching 101: The Coach's Start-Up Kit

This tee ball player is looking to her coach for instructions.

Preface: Play Ball!

As cofounder and president of the T•BALL USA Association, the national nonprofit youth sports organization dedicated to the development and support of the game, I am often asked, "What is tee ball?" Before you start to learn how to be a successful coach, you may need to add to your knowledge of the sport. Here is some background information.

Tee ball is the entry sport to baseball and softball for youngsters generally aged 4 to 8 years old and has become a major youth recreational activity. Members of two teams take turns hitting a ball off a batting tee set on home plate. Batters try to get on base and advance to home; fielders try to prevent that from happening. The elimination of pitching and any fear of being hit by a pitched ball allows organized team participation at an early age. Young players learn the fundamentals and develop baseball skills in minimally competitive league play. The emphasis is on hitting, running, fielding, and throwing in an active game that combines fun and teamwork.

Branch Rickey, the owner of the Brooklyn Dodgers in the early 1950s, is credited with the introduction of a flexible batting tee made from an automobile radiator hose. It was used for practice by the great stars of that era, such as Jackie Robinson, Duke Snyder, and Gil Hodges. Rules for a tee-based game followed, and using a tee adapted from an inflation cup (a cow-milking device), the sport was widely played in Canada during the 1960s. For many years, Little League Baseball has offered tee ball as an early learning experience for basic baseball skills, and the sport provides a natural transition to their minor league program. Other national and regional youth baseball organizations include tee ball in their programs, including the Cal Ripken Division of Babe Ruth Baseball, the Shetland and Pinto Leagues of PONY Baseball, the Farm League in Dizzy Dean Baseball, and the A Division of Dixie Youth Baseball. (For contact information, see the resources section.)

YMCA sports programs and municipal park and recreation departments in communities of all sizes were early organizers or providers for local league play and continue to be an important part of the game. Many U.S. military bases around the world offer tee ball to families. A growing number of independent, nonaffiliated groups (often parent-established and parent-managed groups) have created and fostered the growth of tee ball in their localities and bring a special vitality and passion to the game.

Tee ball games are played in city parks, youth baseball facilities, and

Tommy Lasorda on Tee Ball

In my years with the Dodger organization, I have had opportunities to watch youngsters learn about the game, teamwork, and life. Tee ball is a fabulous way to introduce the game and to develop the personal skills and attitudes that can mean success in sports and life.

Tommy Lasorda, Los Angeles Dodgers

suburban recreational areas, on grass and turf, from hard-baked sandlots to the lush green South Lawn of the White House.

Tee ball programs are offered in every state, most territories, and internationally. The U.S. constituency includes league organizers, administrators and staff, coaches, managers, volunteers, youth sports officials, local sponsors, and the friends, parents, and players from the nearly 18 million families with boys and girls of tee ball age. As the game is the first organized sport for many children, there is a very high level of family involvement and participation.

Local groups often develop their own playing rules; until recently, there has been no total standardization of the regulations and equipment, but now the game can be played in a similar manner throughout the country by all types of youth-oriented organizations. The major differences in play concern winning and losing and what constitutes an inning. Many leagues position the game as a learning experience that is fun, builds skills and a sense of teamwork, features excitement for all, and has no winner or loser. Other leagues do keep score and have one team win. Some leagues consider an inning to be the traditional three outs; most prefer the *bat-around* version, where an inning ends after every player on each team has batted once. The *coach-pitch* version, where an adult throws the ball to the batter, is becoming increasingly popular for older players whose hitting skills are more developed. Generally, communities will determine the best regulations for their own games. T•BALL USA has developed recommended rules of play (see page 27) based on the advice and experience of many organizers, administrators, coaches, and parents from successful tee ball programs in all parts of the country. However the game is played, it is a proven way for children to have fun, develop basic skills, and learn to play together on a team.

Parents who become coaches receive memorable benefits from their involvement in the sport. Beyond the photographs and videos, there is an irreplaceable bond formed between the young players and the moms and dads who work with them on the field of play and at home. This book was written to help you maximize the opportunity to instruct a team of children and to enjoy the experience. You may always remember the first time a little kid with a glove looks up and calls you "Coach."

President George W. Bush, at the May 6, 2001, opening-day event of the Tee Ball on the South Lawn program, said, "I want to thank coaches all across America who take time out from their busy schedules to teach the importance of teamwork and playing by the rules."

Introduction: So You Said You'd Be the Coach, Huh?

It sounded easy. Your kid came home and said some other kids were "gonna play tee ball." You probably thought enrolling your child was a great idea. Your youngster would learn to play a team sport, make new friends, get some exercise, and spend less time in front of the TV or playing computer games. You would have some free hours every week to work on your "to-do" list. Wrong! When you went to the league sign-up you found out that the team needed a coach. You volunteered—why not? After all, you know the basics of baseball; how hard could it be? Now you realize that there's a lot to learn about how to instruct young children in the fundamentals and basic skills of the game in a way that will keep their attention and provide both fun and personal rewards for every player—and yourself.

You're a baffled parent. But don't worry. This book will help you train a team of young athletes. You need to know the rules and procedures of the game. You'll have kids who've never played a team sport, some who have (perhaps soccer), and some who may have already played tee ball. You'll have to work around the differences in age, size, capability, concentration, and attitude. You'll have to deal with other parents. These matters and other game-related factors are covered in this book.

If your child previously played tee ball, you may already be an experienced tee ball parent. Perhaps you were a volunteer and helped with the equipment, car pools, postgame snacks, or other related tasks. But now you're the coach, and there's a lot more to learn. This book's for you.

How to Use This Book

Coaching Tee Ball: The Baffled Parent's Guide is a blend of basic information, preseason essentials, skill development, drills, practice recommendations, game-time actions, and reference materials. You can read the book from cover to cover or refer to specific sections as needed.

Part One, Coaching 101: The Coach's Start-Up Kit, will navigate you through the essential preseason activities and take you through a game. Do you want to learn the elements of effective coaching? Chapter 1, Creating an Atmosphere of Good Habits, includes them. Do you need to review the general rules of the game? Chapter 2, Before Hitting the Field: Tee Ball in a Nutshell, will provide the essential information, including the positioning of the players, what happens when the ball is in play, game variations, and the coach's responsibilities. Administrative and off-the-field matters, including equipment, are presented in chapter 3, Setting Up the Season. Chapter 4, Essential Skills—and How to Teach Them, covers principles of batting, fielding, throwing, and running. Chapter 5, The Practice, centers on one of your most important coaching responsibilities—skill development. Drill suggestions for both beginning and advanced players are presented in chapter 6,

Sample Practices. Your responsibilities before, during, and after a league game are covered in chapter 7, Game Time. Chapter 8, Dealing with Parents, Gender Issues, and Safety and Health, provides advice on handling these areas.

Part Two, Drills: The Foundation for Development, Success, Happiness, and a Coach's Peace of Mind, is a storehouse of proven drills for quality tee ball play. There are three kinds of drills: Warm-Up (W), Defensive (D), and Batting (B). Chapter 9, Warm-Up Drills: Throwing, Fielding, and Baserunning, presents 33 skill-developing activities. Chapter 10, Defensive Drills: Infield Play, Outfield Play, and Team Defense, offers specific drills for when the team is on the field. Need some imaginative drills for hitting? See chapter 11, Batting Drills. Parents should be encouraged to help their kids practice away from the playing field, so chapter 12, At-Home Drills, outlines throwing, catching, running, and hitting drills that can be done at home or in any open recreational area.

The drills in this book are based on information provided by experienced coaches from successful tee ball programs around the country. You don't have to run them exactly as described. League policies differ, practice field limitations may exist, and kids (and teams) will have varying attitudes toward certain practice components. Some players just want to bat, some don't want to run, and some don't even want to be there. Remember, you're the coach. Feel free to be creative and to adapt any of the drills presented in these pages to accomplish your goals.

The questions in the Question and Answer sections all came from other baffled people. Most were e-mail inquiries received at and responded to by T•BALL USA. Others were compiled from a questionnaire sent to representative tee ball programs about frequently asked questions. The sidebars were provided by experienced members of the tee ball community and offer useful information and tips. The photographs illustrate specific actions and activities described in the text, and portray the spirit of the game. The appendix includes a recent survey that offers information on building successful tee ball programs, a description of T•BALL USA, a coaching checklist, a glossary, and a resource section. The index will help you quickly locate specific topics within the book.

A Word on Coaching

Over the years at T•BALL USA, we've watched and heard about a broad spectrum of tee ball coaches: the good, the bad, the experienced, the novice, the prepared, the untrained, the qualified, the unfit, the thoughtful, the impatient, the neat, the sloppy, the firm, the easy-going, the loud, the moderate, the productive, the failed, the satisfied, the frustrated, the physically active, or the comparatively passive. Most coaches are effective, constructive, and dependable and provide a positive influence for the youngsters on their

The coach prepares the batter to hit the ball off the tee.

team. Many return every year that their children play tee ball. Some remain active in the sport even after their own kids have outgrown the game. With few exceptions, almost all coaches are parents and amateurs. From this mix of personalities, individual characteristics, and abilities, are there procedures

Major League Baseball and Tee Ball

Major League Baseball supports grassroots programs that encourage participation by children of all ages and abilities. Tee ball, which can serve as a bridge between instructional and live pitching, is a successful example of such grassroots efforts, giving boys and girls at an early age the opportunity to learn and enjoy the game of baseball.

Thomas C. Brasuell, Vice President, Community Affairs, Major League Baseball

and knowledge generally used by the most successful coaches? Yes. Here are ten recommended coaching actions from experienced coaches.

1. **Realize that kids have separate needs, different responses to instruction, and varying abilities to learn skills.** You may need to modify your teaching methods to handle specific individual situations and abilities.

2. **Prepare and organize.** A written schedule of activities and drills will make practices more productive. Allow time to work with individuals and small groups. Stick to the schedule.

3. **Have as many practices as possible.** This is especially important before the season begins and early in the season.

4. **Get help.** Assistants and volunteers can lighten your workload. High school baseball players can be especially useful, as they minimize the generation gap between the kids and adult coaches. For advice, talk to other coaches in your league, from other leagues, and from other youth sports.

5. **Work closely with the team manager.** Your manager may be able to assume responsibility for matters concerning schedule adjustments, equipment, playing field conditions, and various administrative functions.

6. **Make parents aware of the rules and league policies.** Be sure that they fulfill their responsibilities before, during, and after practices and games, such as arriving on time, on- and off-field assignments, snack time, and at-home practice.

7. **Simulate defensive play situations.** Put your players' skills to use in practice sessions and enhance their teamwork.

8. **Practice patience.** Be aware that patience is more than a virtue—it's the key to success.

Opportunity and Reward

Children have played baseball since the game was invented and, although the highest level of the game—and the most visible—is played by grown men, it is still a kid's game. Even the pros will admit this.

The level of play has increased in recent years, and records that have stood for decades continue to topple. Today's players are bigger, stronger, and faster, and the competition is more intense every step up the ladder. Why is this so? Kids are better trained and start playing earlier. The introduction of very young players to tee ball has had a very real impact on the level of play and skills of dedicated players. There are now adults in Major League Baseball who began playing in tee ball!

As a tee ball coach, you have a wonderful opportunity to accomplish some very important things. First and foremost, you will be introducing a new crop of fledgling baseball players to the game each year, and it will be you who they remember as their first coach. The experience you provide will encourage them to go on or to switch to a different sport. Your job is simply to make it a fun experience.

Next, you will be teaching fundamentals skills, on a very basic level, that will ultimately be the foundation upon which all further skills rely. It is your job to know what you're doing, even if on an elementary level. You must be a student of the game as much as the kids are. Asking questions of seasoned coaches, watching games at higher levels, and reading about coaching will ensure that you have the knowledge you need to succeed as a coach. And by "succeed" I do not mean winning games. I mean making it fun, teaching some skills, and watching your crop of players "age out" and move up to the next level, eager, excited, and ready to continue learning and growing. The early start you give these kids will maximize their chances of success in this wonderful game . . . and years later, when one of them squeaks through the long, circuitous road from youth baseball to high school to college and finally to professional baseball, you'll feel a sense of pride for a job well done. And tickets will be waiting for you at Will Call.

Have fun, teach your players to have fun, and enjoy the experience.

Dave Destler, Publisher and Editor, *Junior Baseball* magazine

9. Keep your players interested. Attention spans vary greatly in the tee ball age group. Cut drills short, if necessary. Have a fun activity in reserve to regenerate interest.

10. Concentrate on skill development. Repetition of the fundamentals is essential and makes a good coach great.

Babe Ruth said, "Start them when they're young. Teach them to play when they're four years old." Organized tee ball has responded in a meaningful manner, providing an avenue for boys and girls to begin their baseball experience and establish a pattern of participation and pleasure for years to come. Tee ball is a game for the entire family and the community to enjoy. It provides special satisfaction and fulfillment for the adults who coach the teams. Play ball!

Coaching 101:
The Coach's Start-Up Kit

CHAPTER 1

Creating an Atmosphere of Good Habits

The perception of you as a competent and experienced coach can mask the reality of your "rookie" status if you project an image of confidence, authority, and control right from the beginning of your coaching career. It's essential that your role be clearly understood by the players and parents, and that they know what you expect from them in return. Establish positive relationships and maintain announced procedures. After the first team meeting and several practice sessions, your capabilities and skills will develop, as will your personal style of instruction.

Establish Your Identity as Coach

First impressions count: Be sure that you look the part of a coach. Chino slacks or shorts and collared polo shirts are better for your image than jeans and T-shirts. Use a clipboard for your Practice Session Worksheet (see pages 52–53) and game-time notes. Wear a whistle. Use a small chalkboard; school-age children respond well and remember visual images. Tell the kids (including your own), the parents of your players, and all persons involved with your team to call you "Coach."

Be a Good Communicator

You'll have to deal with the reality of short attention spans and lapses of interest that are common among children of tee ball age. Try to keep your instructions clear, simple, and uncomplicated. Tee ball is, after all, child's play. Avoid complex or multitask directions. Your coaching tactics may need to be adapted for different learning abilities.

It's essential that the players' parents know how the game is played. A summary of the basic rules is included in chapter 2 for their reference. Most players want to know the rules, too. A kid-friendly listing is on page 26. You can adapt these tools to conform with your league's regulations and playing procedures.

Cal Ripken Jr. on Tee Ball

Sports can be such a healthy vehicle for kids, but the key is the behavior of the coaches and parents. First and foremost, make sure the kids are having fun and enjoying it. This is vital to their long-term commitment to and enjoyment of sports. Also, be consistent. If you are always cheering them when they are having some success, don't become quiet or have a negative reaction when they struggle. Also, make sure that all of the kids participate, not just the most talented ones.

Cal Ripken Jr., former third baseman and shortstop, Baltimore Orioles;
member, The Sports Authority Celebrity Coach's Corner Advisory Board

Expectations

Youngsters excel when the goal is something they believe they can achieve. Every child needs to know what you envision for the team and what you expect from the players as individuals. At the beginning of the season, it's important to establish achievable objectives: learning new skills; trying their best; developing teamwork; exhibiting good behavior; practicing at home; respecting teammates, coaches, umpires, and other teams; pre-

When preparing a batter to hit off the tee, it is important to be at eye level with the player.

senting a positive attitude; showing concern for safety; demonstrating enthusiasm; and having fun. Reaching for, meeting, or exceeding your stated goals will generate self-esteem, pride, and a lasting sense of accomplishment in the kids. You'll feel pretty good, too.

Method

You'll discover that youngsters respond better when they have a good sense of what tee ball activities each practice will involve. Establish a routine for practices (for more on practices, see chapters 5 and 6). Try to maintain the same schedule throughout the season. Leave room for flexibility within the overall plan; the team will quickly let you know which drills are more fun, and you can switch to these drills if players seem to be losing interest or when a change of pace is needed. Your league may not identify a winner and a loser; most don't for the youngest players. Nevertheless, on game day there will be two teams playing—each one trying to make hits and get on base and trying to prevent the other team from doing so. There's always an undercurrent of competition. The parents may express it more directly than the kids. Have your players focus on doing well, using their new skills, playing fair and as a team, and having fun. Their sense of competition can be minimized until such time as they play under rules where runs count and scores are kept.

Effective coaching is built on the blending of many elements, including the following "P-words."

Preparation. If you haven't done your homework, your team can't progress. You need to get ready for meetings with your team and their parents, work out in advance the components of each practice session, ensure that your assistants and volunteers are available and understand their assignments, check with the team manager or responsible adult on matters regarding the field of play and equipment, resolve any outstanding problems before the next practice or game, and try to anticipate the unexpected.

Patience. Some kids require a great deal of repetition before they master a sports skill. You need to have the staying power to endure the time spent describing, demonstrating, and correcting the actions required for children to hit and field with some degree of competence. It takes time for youngsters and a team to build self-esteem and confidence in their ability to learn and play the game. Patience is the foundation for skill development and motivation. Your patience will be rewarded.

Poise. Self-composure is essential. Suppress any frustrations; yelling is not effective and seldom brings long-term results. If your physical and verbal conduct remain calm in times of stress, your team will see you as "cool," the ultimate designation from their age group. Your relationship with other parents will likely involve diplomacy and consideration. During games, remember that mistakes happen. Be fair and cooperate with the umpires.

Praise. When a player or the team earns your approval, this should be publicly recognized. There's no more effective way to motivate than a few spontaneous or planned words of congratulation. Make sure the parents hear your comments directly or learn about any compliments their child received. Praise is not limited to actions fully accomplished. Calling out "Good try!" immediately recognizes effort, rewards the individual player, and inspires the entire team.

The Coach

The importance of a competent coach cannot be overstated. A youth league coach may be the second or third most influential person in a young sports participant's life, behind a parent or a teacher. A properly trained coach can make a significant difference in a young child's personal and game skills. A coach can also make the game *fun*, keeping more children active longer.

Abraham Key, President and CEO, PONY Baseball and Softball

What We Look For in a Coach

Potential coaches are always out there just waiting to be found! So how do we discover them?

First of all, we find people who are willing to volunteer their time and energy. The best candidates are parents. Second, volunteers need to have two important characteristics: a *positive attitude*, because they will be working with children; and *self-confidence*, because they have to "take charge to be in charge." Once we have identified a prospective coach who has these two essential qualities, then we ask about any previous experience with baseball and any dealings with other people's children. Here are the elements we look for in an interview. Ideally, a coach should

- know or have played baseball or softball

- have some familiarity with tee ball

- have the ability to teach and coach youngsters

- work well with children

- deal effectively with parents

After a coach has been selected and the program has started, an evaluation is necessary. How do we do this? First, we observe the new coach in action. Does the coach explain the fundamentals of tee ball in a format that children can easily understand? Does the coach involve the other parents and adults with the instruction of the children? Is the coach a positive role model?

Next, we evaluate the team's progress. Is the team improving with every practice or each game played? Does the team understand the basics of the game? And, most important, are the children and their parents having a good time and enjoying themselves? Remember, the name of the game is tee ball, and the goal is *fun for everyone!*

Lorrie Greenberg, Commissioner, San Bruno Tee Ball, San Bruno, California

Pep talk. A short meeting with the team before a game is important. The players will already be excited (and apprehensive) about playing another team in front of family and strangers. Your brief speech should be directed to the entire group, not to specific individuals. Tell them to remember what they've practiced, to do their best, to play as a team, and to have fun. Minipep talks can be held during the game while the team is on the bench just prior to their turns at bat. Only positive comments should be made at this time.

Practice. This is where and when the good habits you've instilled are first tested. You'll add other components to your teaching style as your involvement in the sport increases and you get more coaching experience. The patterns and routines you develop will provide confidence and the framework for success for yourself and your team.

Build trust with the players and their families. Your relationship with them will measure your capability and effectiveness as a coach more than big hits and great fielding plays. Most important, enjoy the full tee ball experience.

Before Hitting the Field: Tee Ball in a Nutshell

This chapter introduces you to the basics of tee ball, including important rules, player positioning, and what can happen when the game begins. More specific advice and strategy will come in later chapters, but this should get you started in the right direction.

Recommended Basic Rules and Positioning

Tee ball is the only sport where the ball is put into play by the *offense* and then only handled by the *defense*. The number of defensive players on the field at any one time often exceeds the traditional nine in baseball and softball (see diagram page 14).

The Tee Ball Field

The game does not require a conventional setting; many leagues play on grass in municipal parks and other open areas. The *field of play* (see diagram) is shared by an infield and an outfield and is separated into fair and foul territory. It's similar to a standard youth baseball-softball layout, but there are only 50 feet between the bases. The diamond is a square and has a base at each corner. The center of the pitcher's area is 38 feet from the point of home plate. If there are fences, maximum distance is 115 to 125 feet from the batting tee. The foul lines extend from home plate past first and third base. *Fair territory* is the playing field within and including the foul lines. *Foul territory* is the area outside the foul lines and includes a pie-shaped wedge extending 10 feet out from the batting tee. The *playing line* is an imaginary or marked line running between first base and third base. It can also be an arc, a curved circle section extending out 40 feet from the point of home plate. The *dead ball zone* is an area between home plate and the playing line. (For reduced field dimensions for pre-tee ball, see page 19.)

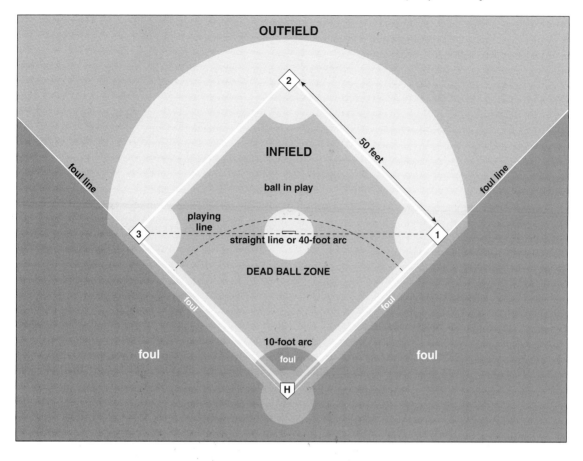

Standard field dimensions.

Infield Positions

"Pitcher": positoned behind the playing line at or near the center of the pitching area.

Catcher: stands at a safe distance behind the batter.

First-Base Player: positioned behind the playing line in fair territory to the right of first base.

Second-Base Player: positioned between first and second base, but closer to second.

Shortstop: positioned between second and third base, but closer to second.

Third-Base Player: positioned behind the playing line in fair territory to the left of third base.

Outfield Positions

Left Fielder: positioned in the outfield between and behind the shortstop and third-base player.

Center Fielder: positioned in the outfield behind second base.

Right Fielder: positioned in the outfield between and behind the first- and second-base players.

Additional Defensive Players

Right Infielder: positioned between the first- and second-base players.

Left Infielder: positioned between the shortstop and third-base player.

Left Center Fielder: positioned between the left and center fielders.

Right Center Fielder: positioned between the right and center fielders.

Deep Left Fielder: positioned behind the left fielder.

Deep Right Fielder: positioned behind the right fielder.

Having more than fifteen players on the field or batting is not recommended. If you have only eight players, eliminate the catcher. Substitutions can be made only after the player to be replaced has played at least one full inning of defense and offense, or in the event of an injury, emotional issue, or a family matter. Reserve players or players no longer in the game should stay on the bench.

Tee ball positions.

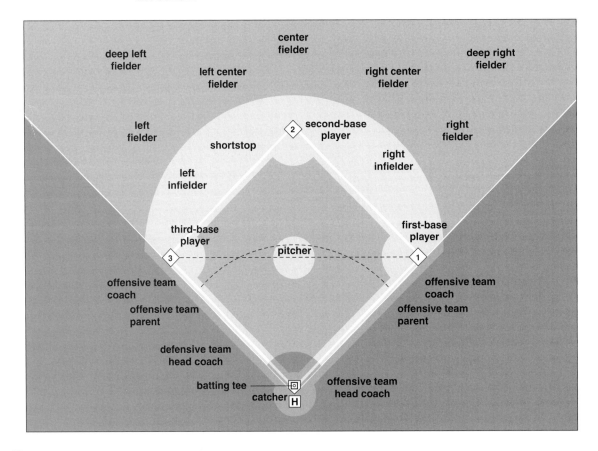

Offensive Players

Players should sit on the bench in batting order. The *at-bat* player (the one who is next to bat) may take a few practice swings in an area away from home plate and the bench.

Object of the Game and General Rules

Members of two teams of nine or more players take turns hitting a ball off a batting tee set on home plate (see diagram). Batters try to get on base and advance to home plate; fielders try to prevent that from happening. In most organized league play with beginning players, scores are not kept, and there are no winners or losers.

The game follows the basic regulations of baseball and softball but has some unique features:

- There's no pitching; the ball is hit off the batting tee.
- There are no strikeouts.
- Since there's no pitching, there are no balls; therefore, there are no bases on balls.
- There's no bunting or half-swings allowed.
- There's no stealing. Base runners can't leave a base until the ball is hit.
- All players on each team bat in each inning of play.
- When a team bats through the batting order once, the team's at-bat half of the inning is over. This is the *bat-around* rule.
- Suggested game length for players ages 6 to 8 is four innings or 90 minutes. The recommendation for younger players (ages 4 to 6) is three innings or one hour. No game should exceed six innings for any reason.
- Unlimited substitutions are permitted, but no player can be taken out of a game unless that player has batted one time and played half an inning in the field.

The Ball Is in Play

When the defensive team is in position and the offensive team members are seated in batting order, the umpire or coach places the ball on the batting tee and calls "Play ball!"

The player stationed in the pitching area acts as an infielder and stays in place until the ball is hit.

All the other infielders stay in their positions and can't cross the playing line until the ball is hit. If a player crosses the line, the umpire calls "Time!," and the ball is dead and returned to the batting tee.

The batter cannot touch the tee (the coach or umpire can adjust the tee to the player's height).

After the ball is successfully put into play and the batter has started to run, the catcher moves up to cover home plate.

A batted ball results in the batter either reaching first base safely or being called *out* by an umpire, manager, coach, or volunteer acting as a ruling official.

A *fair ball* is a batted ball that

- lands in or is touched by a player in fair territory
- bounces past first or third base on or over fair territory
- first lands in foul territory, then rolls into the infield
- bounces on a base or touches a player or an umpire while in fair territory

A fairly batted ball.

A *foul ball* is a batted ball that

- lands and remains in foul territory
- touches a player or umpire in foul territory
- rolls untouched into foul territory before reaching first or third base and comes to rest there

In tee ball, a foul ball is also one that travels less than 10 feet from home plate or a ball that falls off the tee when the batter hits the tee instead of the ball. In either event, the ball is placed on the tee again, and the player continues to swing until the ball is hit into fair territory.

How a Batter Makes an Out

A batter can be called out in several ways. A *ground out* occurs when a batted ball is picked up by a defensive player who, most often, throws the ball to a teammate; the teammate then reaches the base before the hitter arrives there. (Sometimes, the fielder can complete the out without involving another defensive player.) An out is also made when a defensive player *tags* (touches) the batter with the ball or with the ball in the glove as the batter runs to the base. A *fly out* occurs when a batted ball is caught by a defensive player before it touches the ground in fair or foul territory.

How a Batter Reaches Base

If a ball isn't caught before it reaches the ground and isn't received at first base before the batter arrives there, the batter has a *single* base hit and may stay safely at first base or try to run to other bases.

If the defensive team can get the ball to second or third base or home plate and touch the base or tag the batter before the batter arrives at that base, the batter is out. A hit that allows the batter to safely reach second base is a *double*; if the batter reaches third base, it's a *triple*. On a *home run*, the batter runs around all the bases and crosses home plate, as do any teammates already on base.

A base can also be gained on an *error* (a defensive player mishandles the ball) or by a *fielder's choice*, which means the defense decides to get an existing runner out while allowing the batter to get on base.

The Base Runner

The batter becomes a base runner if the batter hits the ball into fair territory or a fielder makes an error. The batter goes to first base and the ball is dead if fielder interference is called or if a fair ball strikes a base runner or umpire before the ball passes or touches a fielder. A runner has a right to be at each base by getting there without being put out and can stay until legally advancing to another base or until being forced to leave by another base runner.

A runner must remain on base until the ball is hit. If the runner is off the base when the ball is hit, the runner is out. Two runners can't be on the same base at the same time. The first runner to legally arrive is safe; the other runner may be tagged out. If the first runner is forced to advance but doesn't, the second runner has the right to the base.

How a Base Runner Advances around the Bases

A base runner may advance if a ball is hit into fair territory or thrown into fair or foul territory, after any fly ball is caught (but the runner must first *tag up* by touching the current base), or if a fair ball hits a base runner or umpire after passing or touching a fielder. A runner must return to the base after a ball is caught on the fly, when a foul ball is not caught, or if there is batter, runner, or umpire interference. If a fielder overthrows the ball to a base, the runner is allowed one extra base. There's no *stealing* (attempting to run to the next base during an at-bat situation) in either standard or coach-pitch tee ball.

How a Base Runner Makes an Out

A base runner is called out and prevented from reaching a base if the runner

- is made to advance to another base, and the fielder with the ball tags the runner or touches the base before the runner arrives (called a *force-out*)
- is tagged by a fielder when not standing safely on base when the ball is in play
- passes another runner or arrives last while another runner is on a base
- leaves a base before a fly ball is caught and is tagged before returning
- touches and runs past first base safely, turns toward second, and is tagged
- runs more than 3 feet outside of a direct line between the bases to avoid being tagged (the runner can go outside the base path to avoid obstructing a fielding attempt)
- interferes with a player fielding a batted or thrown ball
- is involved in a *double play* (two offensive players are put out in the same action)
- is hit by a fair ball while off base and before the ball passes any infielder except the pitcher
- misses touching a base, and a defensive player tags the runner or base
- purposely kicks the ball or runs the bases backward

Left: A base runner is forced out by a fielder with the ball tagging the base before the runner reaches it.

Right: A runner is out if tagged by a fielder with the ball.

After players have moved ahead on the bases as far as possible or after an out, the umpire calls "Time!," and puts a ball back on the batting tee.

Game Variations

There are three variations of basic tee ball. These are more frequently offered by independent, nonaligned community groups than by the local affiliates of national youth baseball leagues. Each of these options is structured for a specific phase of the players' development, from the beginning of organized team play to the period prior to the transition to conventional baseball and softball.

Pre-Tee Ball

This program provides an introductory training and playing experience for youngsters not fully ready for regular tee ball. The players are mostly 4- and 5-year-olds whose size, competence, and/or social development make them unable to participate in the standard game. Mature 3½-year-olds may also be eligible for pre-tee ball. A player who becomes too strong for pre-tee ball (one who shows advanced skills and may be a safety risk for others) should be moved up into regular tee ball.

In pre-tee ball the playing field is reduced to 30 feet between the bases, and the outfield is limited to 60 to 75 feet from the batting tee. The center of the pitcher's area is 25 feet from the tee. The imaginary playing line remains between first and third base or within an arc 24 feet from home plate. The foul ball zone is a 5-foot radius from the tee.

Standard tee ball rules are modified for pre-tee ball as follows.

- The minimum number of players per team is eight, the maximum is twelve.
- The game length is three complete innings. A one-hour time limit is recommended.
- The bat-around rule is mandatory.
- The offensive team may have coaches at all the bases and a hitting coach near the tee.
- The defensive team may have three coaches in the infield and three coaches or volunteers in the outfield.
- *Note:* Some rules may be relaxed if the umpire or league organizers believe players are unable to fully participate in the game.

Many 4-year-old players (and younger) have the physical ability and emotional stability to play in an organized team game, but careful and impartial parental participation is required. As a coach, you must keep the focus on the fun involved in the sport experience and the learning of certain skills and teamwork. Keeping score and winning have no place in pre-tee ball.

A pre-tee ball player waiting for a ball to come her way.

Coach-Pitch

A popular and effective variation of tee ball, coach-pitch involves an adult (or mature teenager) throwing the ball to the batter. All of the basic tee ball rules apply, except no batting tee is used. A coach pitches to his or her own team.

The ball can be thrown underhand or overhand; usually, it's thrown in an arc. The defensive player (the pitcher) stands slightly behind and to the side of the coach-pitcher. The catcher or another coach is positioned well behind the batter.

This modification of the game is generally reserved for teams of older players (6 years and up) or for youngsters whose batting skills have advanced. In many leagues, the coach delivers a predetermined number of pitches, normally three to five. If the batter is unable to hit the thrown balls, a ball is placed on the tee and the game continues. By first using pitched balls and then the batting tee, if necessary, the player is always able to put the ball into play. Coach-pitch is one step closer to traditional baseball or softball.

Pitching Machine

A growing number of leagues are now using pitching machines with older age groups (6- and 7-year-olds) in games or as a training device for more advanced younger players. It's a level beyond coach-pitch, and under proper control and coach supervision, it's an option for qualified players.

Using a machine that can be adjusted to deliver the ball at an appropriate speed, height, and distance has benefits for both the offensive and defensive teams. It provides each batter the same opportunity and promotes batting confidence as players improve their ability to hit a moving ball. There is no concern that an adult pitcher may be overpowering, intimidating, or inconsistent. The ball will be put into play sooner as a result of the accurate pitching, so game times will be shorter. The defensive team's attention span will be better focused because of the more frequent action. You'll find that use of a pitching machine gives you more time to work with the batters and less concern with your own ability in a coach-pitch setting to continually deliver hittable throws to the plate.

Responsibilities of a Coach during the Game

Game coaching is covered in greater detail in chapter 7, but here are some basics to follow. You're responsible for having all of the defensive players in their correct positions when they take the field each inning. When your team's at bat, you (or an assistant) should call the players to home plate in the correct sequence. Be sure that there are coaches at first and third base and—if available—near second base and in the outfield. Young players often drift away from their positions toward the bases or the foul lines or cluster together; correct their positions as necessary. Safety is always important to keep in mind. Your function is to coach; the parents are there to cheer for their kids and the team. Try to maintain these roles.

Basic Safety Measures

Tee ball is a game played with swinging bats, flying balls, and, often, fixed objects such as backstops and fences. For many participants, it's their first experience as part of an organized team sport using authentic (not toylike) athletic equipment on a public field with spectators watching and various other distractions. Common sense and thinking ahead can help provide safe practice and game conditions. As coach, you need to be aware of potentially dangerous situations and how to avoid injuries. Following are some areas of concern. (For more information on safety and health, see chapter 8, pages 81–84.)

In the ideal safety setting, the defensive team is seated behind a protective fence.

Safety Helmets

Today, few parents allow their children to ride bicycles without wearing helmets. The same thinking applies for tee ball players. Helmets are required for the batter, the on-deck batter, the three base runners, and the catcher, and are recommended for the first- and third-base coaches. You must be vigilant that this rule is followed without exception. Helmets can be color-coded so that players can quickly locate the right size for proper fit before they go to bat.

Communication

Young defensive players trying to catch fly balls often run with their heads up and eyes looking skyward. In this situation, players can collide with teammates or fixed objects. It's important to teach your players to communicate. If two or more players are trying to catch the ball, they should continue until one player calls out, "Mine!," or "I've got it!," and then the other player(s) should move away. Players not involved in the action should warn those going after the ball if they're near a fence or a dangerous area. (See Catching Flies **W9** for practice at calling for the ball.)

Warm-Ups

Oversee stretching and conditioning warm-up exercises before every practice and pregame activity. It's a myth that all children are flexible. It's much better to prevent sport-related injuries by proper stretching rather than treating them after they occur. (See the exercises on page 50.)

Throwing and Catching

To minimize the risk of injuries, players should not stand or walk behind throwers and catchers. Stress eye contact between the participants. If a throw is wild or not caught, the intended receiver should run after the ball and bring it (not throw it) back to continue the drill. Instruct your players to immediately stop throwing when you call "Hold the ball!" and to wait for your instructions.

Batting

Players must be cautioned to keep a safe distance away from any players who may be loosening up or practicing bat swings. A bat can sometimes slip out of a batter's hands, so players and coaches should avoid standing or walking

This player is happy and protected in his safety helmet.

Little League and Tee Ball

Tee ball has been a chartered division of Little League Baseball since the early 1970s and continues to be one of its largest. With about 1 million players ages 5 to 8, the Little League Tee Ball Division is the training ground for future Little Leaguers. Little League also offers Tee Ball Softball.

In Little League Tee Ball, the rules of baseball are modified to suit the skills of younger players. Scores are not kept, and most Little League Tee Ball Leagues use a continuous batting order, and every player plays on defense.

The focus in Little League Tee Ball is on fun, and the development of rudimentary skills, with very little emphasis on the competitive aspects of the game that are present at older age levels. Parents are urged to understand that Little League Tee Ball is a time to nurture their child's love of the game so that it can be better appreciated later in their lives. For many children, this is the first exposure to the concept of teamwork that is the hallmark of Little League.

Little League was chosen to administer President George W. Bush's Tee Ball on the South Lawn program, in which Little League teams are periodically invited to play a game on the South Lawn of the White House.

Little League Baseball, Williamsport, Pennsylvania

behind a batter. Remind players that throwing a bat to the ground after hitting the ball can injure the catcher or umpire; some leagues issue a warning the first time a bat is thrown but remove the player from the game after a second offense.

Running

Baserunning and related drills (see pages 95–96) must be supervised, for young players tend to use this activity to work off tension and express individualism. Excessive pregame running can drain stamina and create unnecessary fatigue. Select one or two running drills and schedule them early in the pregame routine.

Snacks

Eating and drinking (except for frequent water breaks) should be prohibited during pregame warm-ups and during games. Postgame snacks, however, are an integral part of overall tee ball activity. The players look forward to socializing with teammates and rejoining their families.

Inspection

Make sure the field is inspected before each practice and game for objects or conditions that could be hazardous to the participants and spectators.

Questions and Answers

Q. Is there any rule regarding the use of the catcher in tee ball? If not, what is the general practice, and what does the catcher do?

A. The catcher is an important position. The player stands behind the batter at a safe distance. After the ball is hit, an adult (umpire or coach) removes the bat and the tee from the area. The catcher then covers home plate to tag any incoming runners. The catcher doesn't do much fielding because the ball is dead if it doesn't pass the playing line. The pitcher and other infielders recover most of the ground balls. Many kids really want to play catcher.

Q. After getting a hit, does the batter have to stop at first base or continue on to second base?

A. The batter, now a runner, looks to the first-base coach for instructions. The coach either points to second base or puts up his or her hands as a signal for the runner to stop at first base. The coach can also call out what to do, but sometimes other adults are yelling instructions, and the player may hear conflicting commands.

   Most leagues (and the parents!) desire and cheer doubles, triples, and home runs. The reality is that singles usually extend to other bases due to poor fielding, grounders or fly balls not trapped or stopped, bad throws, bobbled catches at the bases, and other mishaps. The runner is often out when trying to stretch a single into extra bases. Nothing in the recommended rules of play limits a batter from continuing as far as possible around the bases. But like many things in tee ball, local consensus decides these matters.

Q. If a batted ball hits a base runner running from second to third base, is the runner out?

A. In tee ball, a runner must remain on base until the ball is hit; if off the base when the ball is hit, the runner is out. In the situation you describe, if the runner left second base after the ball was hit and is struck by a fair ball before it passes or touches a fielder other than the pitcher, the ball is dead. The batter goes to first base, and the runner returns to second. If the ball has gone past a fielder, the base runner can advance. This is a difficult play for an umpire to call. Many leagues do not even address this matter in their rules but usually allow the batter to run to first base (with the possibility of being thrown out) and the player hit by the ball to keep moving ahead (with the possibility of being tagged or thrown out).

Q. In standard tee ball, if the ball is hit off the tee and doesn't travel 10 feet, it's a foul. In coach-pitch, if the hit ball (or a bunt) doesn't go more than 10 feet, is it still considered a foul?

A. Yes. In both situations, a ball hit less than 10 feet is a foul ball. Also, there is no bunting in any version of tee ball play. These rules are primarily for the safety of the defensive players.

Q. What can I tell a parent who wants to know the league height for the tee?

A. There is no designated official height. The coach (or a designated adult) adjusts the batting tee for each player based on the height of the batter. The recommended level is to have the ball opposite the player's belly button.

Why I Coach

A passion for athletics has existed in me as far back as I can remember, and along the way I have been influenced by many coaches. I coach because I want to share all of the *positive* lessons and skills that were taught to me. Coaches, like parents and teachers, can play such a vital role in the development of young minds. By giving high fives, wiping teary eyes, instilling positive values, and stressing good sportsmanship, I know I am teaching the same valuable lessons taught to me by those men and women I called "Coach."

Mark Bryson, Head Coach, MLB All-Star FanFest

Tee Ball Rules for Kids

A great way to involve kids right from the beginning is to hand out copies of the following at your preseason meeting. Ask parents to go over the list with their child.

For Kids

Tee ball is a baseball game for young boys and girls. It is a way to have fun while learning how to play. Here are some important things to remember:

- The ball is not pitched to you. It is hit off a batting tee.
- Every player bats and plays in the field.
- There are no strikeouts or walks.
- There is a real or pretend playing line between the first and third bases, or curved 40 feet from home plate.
- No fielder can cross the playing line until the ball has been hit.
- The ball must be hit 10 feet or it is a foul.
- After you hit the ball, don't throw the bat.
- Runners must stay on base until the ball is hit. There is no stealing (running before the ball is put into play).
- An inning is over when all the players on each team have batted.
- A safety helmet must be worn when at bat or on base.

Listen to your coaches. Your league may have some different rules, like keeping score or having a coach pitch to the batter. That's part of the game, too.

Remember, have fun and be a good team player!

Tee Ball Rules for Parents

Here is a brief outline of the basic rules and equipment specifications as recommended by T•BALL USA. Although the rules and specifications are directed to coaches, parents will find them useful as well. Make copies of these to hand out to parents at your preseason meeting (see page 29)

Is there more than one way to play? Yes; variation possibilities are marked with an asterisk (*). Check with your league to learn which rules apply in the game you're coaching.

- Players range from 4 to 8 years old.

- A team can have up to twenty players.

- On the field, a team is allowed a minimum of eight players and a maximum of fifteen.

- Bases are spaced 50 feet apart.

- A real or imaginary playing line is between first and third base, or an arc 40 feet from home plate.

- Every player bats and plays in the field.

- The ball is hit off a batting tee; there is no pitching.*

- There are no walks or strikeouts.

- A batted ball must travel 10 feet or it is a foul.

- No fielder may cross the fielding line until the ball is hit.

- Stealing is not allowed. The runner stays on the base until the ball is hit.

- An inning is over when all players on each team have batted once.*

- The standard game is four innings.*

- Scores are not kept for younger players and, often, not in any tee ball play.

- Safety helmets must be worn.

- Bats are 25 to 26 inches long, are $2\frac{1}{4}$ inches in diameter, and weigh 17 to 20 ounces.

- Game balls are 9 to $9\frac{1}{4}$ inches in circumference, $2\frac{3}{4}$ inches in diameter, and softer than a baseball. Practice balls are the same size and are even softer.

- Gloves range from 9 to 12 inches.

CHAPTER 3

Setting Up the Season

Your responsibilities as a coach will frequently extend well beyond providing instruction to a group of sometimes inattentive or tired or thirsty or bored or, more often, excited and proud and happy youngsters. Depending on the structure and experience of the game's organizing group, you may occasionally perform the functions of a league administrator, team manager, family guidance counselor, teacher, mentor, guru, peacemaker, equipment handler, driver, safety director, logistics expert, and supervisor of well-meaning volunteers. The key to ensure that you and your team have a positive, fun-filled sports experience is *preparation*.

League Policies and Procedures

Research the league prior to the season to make sure it's the right fit for you as far as its positions on such topics as competition, game variations, and the role of parents. It's important to attend coaches' orientation and training sessions to know the league's expectations and regulations (player age requirements, tryout system, team assignment procedure, number of games in the season, expected behavior, policy on awards, etc.). Study the rules of play. Remember that your players and their parents will model your actions; if you follow the accepted guidelines, it's more likely that they will, too.

Practice and Game Schedules

Have a plan for each meeting with your team. It will keep you on track and make the most of the limited time you have with them. Choose times to practice that you'll be able to make without conflict. Try to keep practices on the same days of the week and at the same time all season; it's easier for families to commit to a consistent schedule than one that varies.

If possible, schedule two practice sessions a week before the playing season starts. Once the games have begun, one practice a week may be sufficient. This will provide an opportunity to build on the game-time experiences.

Meet with Parents

Before you hold your first practice, prepare to meet with the full group of team parents or a responsible adult family member, guardian, or friend of each player. At this initial meeting you can discuss goals and expectations of parents, the program, and the coaching staff. Emphasize that tee ball is a fun and active game with the focus on *fun*. Explain the league policies (such as keeping score, winning and losing, game variations, behavior), basic rules and procedures, practice and game schedules, cancellations, reschedules, and emergencies. Provide details about equipment needed, uniforms, and snacks. Some parents won't be familiar with the game of tee ball, so demonstrate how the batting tee works and pass around some tee balls. Distribute handouts covering the key topics discussed, including the rules for kids and parents (see sidebars on pages 26 and 27). This is a good time to hand out the practice and game schedules and your preseason letter to parents (see sample next page). Be ready for questions. This is also the best time to establish a practical communications and contact list and to recruit assistant coaches and volunteers for other responsibilities. (For more on volunteers, see the sidebar on page 31.)

If any parents are unable to attend the meeting, call them afterward, introduce yourself, and summarize what you covered at the meeting. Learn their expectations and apprehensions, if any. Answer their questions. Be sure they know where and when the first practice will take place. Mail them copies of the handouts.

Finding Assistants

You'll need help at practices and before, during, and after each game. Your best source is the parents. As alternatives, consider enlisting high school or college baseball or softball players. They can be very effective working with younger children and have the ability and energy to supervise drills and be on the field with the players during game play action. Assistants can coach at first and third base, facilitate the batting order, monitor for safety, and give parents tips for at-home skill development. Find people you feel comfortable

Set the Ground Rules with Your Assistants

Make sure that you explain your philosophy and expectations for performance and perspective during the season, not only to your players and their parents but to your assistants as well. You don't want to be out on the field with someone who doesn't share your thoughts and convictions about good sportsmanship, patience, and keeping things fun. Your views should be made clear before the season starts.

Sample Preseason Letter to Parents

Dear Parents:

It's almost time for tee ball. My name is [fill in], and I am coach of the [fill in team name]. I am looking forward to a fun-filled season where the kids will improve their skills and learn the values of teamwork, sportsmanship, and fair play. My goal is to create a positive, supportive environment so that every player has a great experience. Regardless of ability, every member of the team deserves to be encouraged. Players should respect each other on the field as they engage in friendly competition and off the field as well. I look to you to help reinforce these important concepts. When you come to practices and games, please limit your contact with the children to positive support from a distance. During games, treat the officials, the other players, the opposing team, and the families and spectators with respect. We are our children's most important role models. I'll set as good an example as I possibly can, and I'd greatly appreciate it if you could do the same.

I have a few "ground rules" I would like to share with you.

- Being on time is critical. Always arrive at games 30 minutes before game time so we have ample opportunity for a team meeting and warm-up.
- Please notify me if your child will not be attending a game or practice.
- For the safety of our children, each child must have a parent (or responsible adult) present at all games and practices. Please do not enlist the coaches. We're working with the entire team and cannot monitor individual kids while instructing the team.
- Each player should bring a 9- to 12-inch broken-in glove and a water bottle and should wear sneakers with flat soles or soft cleats. All personal items must be labeled with your child's name.
- Please give your child a light meal before practices and games. There will be no food allowed in the dugout or on the bench. Also, no distractions (such as GameBoy, Pokemon cards, etc.) are allowed.
- The postgame snack is an important element to the overall experience. Planning the refreshments with the other parents (contact the team Snack Coordinator) is a great way to get involved with the team. It's important to let the Snack Coordinator know if your child has any food allergies.
- Encourage your child! If he or she is trying, always say "Nice try!" Praise your child's progress, and keep the focus on fun.
- If your child doesn't want to participate in a practice or game, he or she won't be required to do so. Let me know if there are any special needs, allergies, or concerns. We'll work together to make tee ball an enjoyable experience for your child.

We're looking forward to a great tee ball season. If you have any questions or concerns, please do not hesitate to call me.

[your name]
[address]
[phone number]
[e-mail, if available]

Calling All Volunteers!

There are parents and family friends who want to support the league and help the team, but who can't participate in field-of-play activities. Their interest and enthusiasm should be encouraged and channeled into administrative responsibilities that are important to a successful tee ball program.

Phone Tree

Whenever you have a message to get out to team members (such as a canceled practice or game, a change of time or place), you call a designated person (the Head Operator) who has arranged a chain of communication—the phone tree. After you make your call, your announcement is quickly and efficiently relayed to the rest of the team.

Transportation

A volunteer (the Carpool Chief) can be responsible for checking that every player has a ride to and from practices and games. Some teams break their roster into small groups of players who live near each other, with one parent making sure that each player in their group is picked up from each practice and game. Be certain parents realize that if they provide a ride for another child, they should watch out for that child during the practice or game.

Refreshments

Young players look forward to a postgame or postpractice activity, usually centered on snacks. This is when they're reunited with family and friends and can mix with the opposing team. They're hungry and thirsty, and they view the occasion as both a reward and an extension of their sports experience. Designate a volunteer (the Snack Coordinator) to create a schedule for families to assist with snack procurement, delivery, and cleanup. The event is best held near the playing field, but sometimes (such as at the end of the season) the team can meet at a local restaurant after the game for food, beverages, or ice cream.

Fund-Raising

Teams often need money for such items as equipment, printed material, mailings, uniforms, awards, photographs, trips, or special events. Find a parent with good community connections to be the Financial Wizard who can develop the means (or delegate others) to raise funds to cover the costs of these activities.

Bench Monitor

Rotate the role of Dugout Dad/Mom/Friend among your volunteers. At each game, have one volunteer stationed with the players as they sit on the bench. This volunteer has several responsibilities: making sure the players go to the tee promptly in the proper sequence and wearing a safety helmet, keeping the players seated when they're not on the field, encouraging players to root for their teammates, and keeping other parents away from the bench.

having in charge in your absence. Your assistants should be a complementary fit to your personality and coaching style.

Number of Players on the Team

Every member of the team who comes to a game plays offense and defense in every inning. See chapter 2 for details on how to position eight to fifteen players in the field for defense; everyone bats each inning.

Equipment

Tee ball requires minimal equipment. The league or game organizers are responsible for bats, practice and game balls, batting tees, three throw-down bases and home plate, safety helmets, benches, and a first-aid kit. Players are responsible for their own gloves. As coach, it's a good idea to have a few extra gloves available. Some players will arrive with other personal items (such as bats, batting gloves, sun or protective glasses, water bottles), and these must be marked with the player's name and home phone number. You'll need a clipboard for the team roster, the batting order, notes for position rotation, and a checklist (see the appendix). Wear a watch and have a whistle.

Balls

A recommended tee ball.

The game tee ball measures between 9 and 9¼ inches in circumference (approximately 2¾ inches in diameter) and weighs between 4 and 5 ounces. Softer than a standard baseball, it may have a molded vinyl core or a sponge rubber center and a stitched leather or synthetic cover. An even softer ball of the same size or larger is often used for individual and team practice sessions. Balls are usually white with red stitching, but balls in color are allowed.

Bat

The bat is a smooth, rounded stick of wood (not laminated) or hollow metal (aluminum or other alloys) 25 to 26 inches long and 2¼ inches in diameter, maximum. It weighs 17 to 20 ounces. Handles may have rubber grips or be taped.

There is a wide selection of reasonably priced bats available. Lighter-weight bats provide better control and a faster swing.

Batting Tee

The game tee is a two-piece metal rod with heavy-duty rubber tubing to support the ball mounted on an institutional-grade rubber base. Most tees can be adjusted up to 34 inches. Lightweight plastic and rubber tees (models with a ball attached to the base with removable nylon cord) are often used for practice.

Gloves

For tee ball, fielders' gloves are constructed of high-quality synthetic leather or other easily flexed materials. A 9-inch glove is recommended for younger or smaller players, a 10-inch glove for the older or larger players. A fielder's glove should never be more than 12 inches long. The first-base player and catcher may use a glove, or a *mitt*, which has no fingers, except for the thumb.

The tee is adjustable so the ball can be properly positioned to the height of each batter.

Tee ball does not require expensive gloves, but the right size is important. Finger control is necessary, so smaller gloves are recommended.

Safety Helmets

Safety helmets are essential pieces of equipment.

Although standard tee ball play involves no pitching (or with mature players, involves a ball coach-pitched in a friendly manner), organizers, coaches, parents, and children should not let this lull them into a feeling that helmets are not important. They are essential. Helmets must be made of high-impact plastic, be fully lined for comfort, and fully protect the head all around, including the temples and ears. Check to see that helmets meet NOCSAE (National Operating Committee on Standards for Athletic Equipment) performance standards. A helmet needs to be the correct size for the player and must not come off during batting or base running. Batters, the on-deck (next to hit) batter, and all base runners must wear safety helmets; they are recommended for the two base coaches.

Throw-Down Bases

It's a good idea to have some throw-down (movable) bases on hand for practice time in case your regular tee ball field is not available. The most practical lightweight bases are 12 inches square and made of PVC plastic. They are usually sold in sets that include three bases and a home plate. Heavy-duty bases are larger and made of rubber. Suggest that families acquire bases to share for at-home fielding and running drills.

Extra throw-down bases allow more kids to participate in running and fielding drills during practices.

Uniforms

Your league may require a full uniform for each player. This consists of a baseball-style jersey, pull-up pants or shorts, high socks, and a baseball cap. Many programs outfit their teams with T-shirts and matching caps. The responsibility for securing uniforms will often be undertaken by a designated parent. Most sporting goods stores have a team sports department or specialist to handle the requirements. Be sure to start early and allow enough time to obtain uniforms (especially those with names or logos or sponsor identification screened on the shirts), as many teams will be ordering during the same period of time. All players should try on their uniforms before the first game to make sure that the fit is right.

Players should save their uniforms for games. At practices, they should dress in active sports apparel: T-shirts, shorts or jeans, and caps. Athletic footwear with flat soles or soft, molded cleats is recommended. Check before each practice and game that no players are wearing jewelry, watches, or metal objects.

Questions and Answers

Q. Our program does not include the use of helmets. Should I be concerned about this?

A. Almost every successful tee ball program requires that a safety helmet be worn (at a minimum) by the batter and the base runners. Try to convince your group to reconsider their position. Cost should not be a factor; safety is the issue. Also, the league's insurance premium may be reduced if helmets are worn.

Q. What is the difference between a manager and a coach?

A. The manager is responsible for the organization and implementation of the team's operations before, during, and after the season. This can include maintaining the team's relationship with the league or local organizing group, securing locations for practices and games, setting up and running meetings with the parents, arranging practice and game schedules, distributing information (rules, procedures, insurance coverage, etc.), procuring equipment and uniforms, coordinating volunteer assignments (transportation, snacks and refreshments, awards), handling financial affairs, and securing local sponsors.

Coaches instruct the players in how to play the various positions and perform the necessary skills: fielding, throwing, catching, running, and—of course—hitting off the batting tee. Coaches teach the concepts of teamwork and fair play. They're the most direct link between the league and the parents. Managers and coaches share certain responsibilities (such as getting volunteers and assistant coaches, resolv-

Coaches and Parents: A Winning Combination

This being our 30th season, the Bolingbrook Tee Ball Association is feeling strong. With nearly 800 kids and 54 teams, ours is a program with a long history of wonderful volunteers and dedicated parents.

As president, one of my duties is to secure coaches for our league. Knowing that our league runs on "volunteer power," I want to find the best coaches I can. Fortunately, tee ball is an entry-level program, and thorough knowledge of baseball is not necessary. Then what is the most important aspect of a coach?

I believe that most important is the coach's ability to communicate with the players and the parents. Parents want to be informed of everything going on with the team and the league. They want to know when games and practices are scheduled. They want to know the philosophy of the coach: where he or she stands on things like winning, fun, fundamentals, and sportsmanship.

They want to know what they can do for the team, how to support their child, and how to make the best of their family's experience.

In addition, it is important for the head coach to let the parents know what he or she expects of them. Attendance at practices, practicing at home, helping at games and practices—all of these things are important for the coach to communicate to the parents.

In our league, we strongly encourage parent meetings before the season begins. It is an opportunity not just for the coach to meet the kids and the parents, but a time when all of these issues can be addressed and any questions can be answered. It is a time when the head coach can secure the parents' assistance with all the aspects of the team. A good parent meeting sets the tone for the season.

In my experience, the most successful teams—not necessarily the most winning teams—are the ones with the most parent participation. It's an opportunity for the kids and their families to come together and have some of the best fun they'll ever have.

Carl Crooks, President, Bolingbrook Tee Ball Association, Bolingbrook, Illinois

ing problems, and safety). Basically, managers organize and deal with the off-the-field matters the team needs to have in place to play the sport; the coach is the teacher and motivator.

Q. What should I say when asked what the right age is for a child to start playing?

A. Each child is different physically, emotionally, and socially. If your program is designed with these things in mind, parents should not be afraid to follow its predetermined age structure, even if it's different than what they desired.

Q. Can a child play on my team at a younger age than the other kids if he or she has been playing at home and already developed some skills?

A. Follow the league's age requirements. The atmosphere for a child on a ball field in front of strangers is quite different than that at home with family.

Q. If a child played in our league last season but has since moved out of the area, can the child still play here?

A. This is a matter of league policy, not your decision, so find out what your league allows.

Q. I'm a new coach in a league that keeps score for tee ballers. I'm interested in the pros and cons of keeping score for kids in this age group.

A. Keeping score is often a local decision made by the league administrators and the parents. Leagues that are part of national youth baseball organizations are governed by the rules and procedures of their parent body. In the early years (4- and 5-year-old players) the emphasis should be on learning the basic rules and skills, playing on a team, and having fun. The older kids (6- and 7-year-old players) can generally handle winning and losing, as they see it in other sports, in school games, and on TV. Young players who are mature for their age can compete if they're on teams that balance out the ages and skills of the participants. The wishes of the community should prevail.

CHAPTER 4

Essential Skills— and How to Teach Them

Instructing the basic skills of tee ball requires patience and understanding. Most kids have only a vague grasp of the rules of the game and have had minimal experience playing a team sport. There are physical and mental skills to be taught; both take time.

Your job as coach is to help your players—individually and collectively—learn and practice the fundamentals. The key is to keep each activity a fun experience. Praise enhances enthusiasm.

Watch for the smiles; they're a measure of your success!

Batting

The Principles

Hitting a ball off a tee is the essential element of the game. It's the basis of the sport, as it allows young children to play in an organized team activity without the fear of having a ball thrown to or at them. As in baseball and

Tee Ball Skills

Tee ball provides an opportunity for boys and girls to actively participate in playing baseball under conditions appropriate for their age. It is designed to teach the following skills:

- swinging a bat properly at a ball
- fielding the ball
- throwing the ball
- learning and practicing the game

Each child will have the thrill of hitting the ball and running bases. We hope the whole family will be involved in this true spirit of sportsmanship.

Mel Carpenter, Johnson County Parks and Recreation Department, Shawnee Mission, Kansas

Babe Ruth League and Tee Ball

Tee ball is offered in Cal Ripken Baseball, a division of the Babe Ruth League. The program provides a structured introduction for youngsters to the great game of baseball. Tee ball offers children a chance to play in a noncompetitive environment while learning the skills of hitting, fielding, throwing, and running. The primary goal of the Babe Ruth League is to give every player the opportunity to participate and—most important—to have fun.

Joe Smiegocki, Vice President, Marketing, Babe Ruth League, Trenton, New Jersey

softball, hitting is the most important skill to master. Unless the ball is put into play, there's no need for the other skills. Many players have the most fun batting since it's their opportunity to be the center of attention. Batting requires individual attention; there are different physical and mental elements within every player. As coach, you need to be patient, be positive, and give praise when deserved.

The Grip

The bat is held with hands one on top of the other above the knob. Make sure that the bat is not too long or too heavy for the batter. The bat is gripped firmly and not squeezed. If the child's fingers are long enough, try positioning the hands an inch above the knob to provide better control.

The **grip**. A batter must be comfortable holding the bat. Don't worry about how the knuckles line up as long as the hands keep the bat steady.

The Stance

Adjust the batting tee with the ball set slightly above the hitter's waist. The player faces the tee with the feet spread shoulder-width apart. Both feet point toward the tee; the front foot should be even with the tee. The knees are bent, and the body is in a slight crouch, leaning forward. The weight is on the balls of the feet. Sometimes, a little more weight on the rear foot helps. The batter brings the bat up and away from the body. The hands stop by the rear shoulder, a few inches away from the body. The bat should be pointing up and tilted slightly back. Don't let the bat be held too low; repeat "Hands up!" It's important that the rear elbow does not touch the player's body; if it does, the swing can't

The **stance**. This batter's position is nearly perfect. He only needs to line up his belt buckle opposite the ball, bend his knees, and lift his heels off the ground.

be level. At this stage, the shoulders must be level and the head steady. The body is still—no movement—and the eyes are fixed on the ball.

The Swing

Left: The **swing**. If your batters rotate their bodies, watch the ball on the tee, and keep the bat level as it moves to meet the ball, they'll soon become good hitters.

The player leans slightly away from the tee (with more weight on the rear foot) and then takes a short step forward with the front foot at the start of the swing. Most important: the swing must be level so that the bat makes contact with the center of the ball. The player tries to watch the bat hit the ball and to keep the head down. The batter's weight shifts to the front foot, but the back foot (the toes at least) should stay on the ground. This is difficult for young players but will help their hitting.

The Follow-Through

Right: The **follow-through**. After hitting the ball, the batter should continue the swing so that the bat comes around behind the body.

Both arms extend and continue in motion, completing the swing. Instruct the batters to "hit through the ball" and not to stop the swing on contact. After the ball is hit and the swing completed, the batter must drop (not throw) the bat near the tee.

Fielding

The Principles

In tee ball, there's little difference in the instructions given to infield or outfield players. Your job is to establish and improve good defensive skills. Since most leagues rotate player positions during a game or at some point during the season, each child should be taught the fundamentals. These basics should be reviewed at every practice and, when possible, by the players at home with family. The three "defensive commandments" to emphasize are: keep your eyes on the ball, watch the ball go into the glove, and cover the ball with the other hand.

Ground Balls

The fielders stand with their legs shoulder-width (or wider) apart. Instruct the players to bend their knees, get low, and lean forward. The weight should be on the balls of the feet. The glove is held with the fingers down near the ground. When a ball is hit on the ground, the player runs to the ball and keeps in front of it. The ball can be trapped, scooped, or caught. As soon as the ball is in the glove, the player should cover it immediately with the throwing hand. The glove is then brought up to the body. Tell the fielders not to stand up until the ball is secure in the glove.

This defensive player looks prepared but should be on the balls of his feet, not his heels.

Balls usually do not come directly to a player. Show the fielders how to move to one side or the other and stop the ball with an outstretched glove. Remind them to always stop the ball and cover it before taking the next defensive action.

Many beginning (and some experienced) players are understandably apprehensive about catching an oncoming moving ball—on the ground or in the air. With these players, begin by throwing—not hitting—balls to them from no more than 10 feet away, and gradually increase the distance. When they are comfortable fielding thrown balls, start hitting balls to them, with the players stationed beyond the playing line, or 40 feet away. Begin with ground balls, and gradually introduce fly balls. Practice builds confidence, which reduces or eliminates fear. When you see a previously hesitant fielder running toward a ball, you will know that you have a qualified team player.

Fly Balls

In tee ball, there are frequent pop-ups, which usually provide added excitement to the game. These plays take slightly longer to develop and often draw a crowd of players to where the ball is headed. Several fielders may run to catch it. They should never turn their backs to the ball. The closest fielder to the expected landing spot should call "I've got it!" and the other players should make room for the play. The best technique for young players is for them to stop running and wait for the ball. Sometimes a player lets a ball come down on one side and tries to catch it waist-high. Correct this bad habit, as the ball will usually drop beside the player.

The ball should always be caught with hands together, fingers up, shoulder-high but not over the head. It's important for the fielder to watch the ball go into the glove and to cover it.

You'll see players attempt (only sometimes successfully) one-handed catches. Don't encourage this maneuver.

Thrown Balls

Defensive players get many balls thrown to them, either when they are covering bases or as part of the relay of a ball from another fielder. Poor catch-

Left: This fielder is correctly "charging" a ground ball and is ready to cover it with his bare hand.

Right: This player, waiting to catch a fly ball, demonstrates good technique with his hands above his waist and his head up.

ing is responsible for most defensive misplays, player and team frustration, and parent unrest. However, it is the easiest skill for a kid to practice. All it takes is a little instruction and another person—child or adult. Have your players always watch the ball as it comes toward them. On a ball thrown above a player's waist, the player's hands should be held together facing out with the thumbs up. On a ball coming below the waist, the hands should be together, pointing down with the little fingers touching. This is often called "pinkies down." Keep reminding your fielders to "catch and cover."

Throwing

The Principles

It usually takes young players a long time to develop good throwing form. You want your defensive players to be able to throw straight on a direct line and as hard as they can.

The Grip

The thumb is always under the ball. For players with small hands, the three middle fingers should be over the ball with the little finger off to the side. Players with larger hands should have the index and middle fingers over the ball and the other two on the side. Don't worry if the fingers go along the seams or over them; your players won't take the time or even have the manual dexterity to set their fingers down precisely.

The Motion

The thrower's eyes are focused on the target. Their legs are apart and the foot on the throwing-arm side is set behind the body. When the arm with the ball is brought back and up, the front shoulder is turned toward the intended recipient. Younger and beginning players should angle their throwing arm into an L shape, bent at the elbow. Older and experienced players can use a full arm

Fielding a ball coming to belt level is best caught "pinkies down."

This 4-year-old player's fingers are just long enough to hold the ball correctly for a throw.

Seven Fielding Tips from Coach Tom McClure

Stance should be with feet shoulder-width apart, knees bent, hands in front, and weight on the balls of the feet.

Pinkie fingers should be together on balls coming below the waist.

Thumbs should be together when balls are above the waist.

Watch the ball go into the glove and cover it with the throwing hand.

Charge slow rolling balls.

Pick up stopped ground balls with your bare hand.

Know where to throw the ball.

Tom McClure, Northside Youth Organization, Atlanta, Georgia

extension. The thrower takes a step toward the target with the foot opposite the throwing arm (right-hander on the left foot; left-hander on the right foot). The player pushes off the back foot as the throw begins and ends with weight on the forward foot. The ball is released in front of the body, and the throwing arm follows through down past the waist. When the thrower and the receiver are close to each other, the ball should be thrown underhand. In this case, the throwing hand faces up, all fingers are under the ball, foot placement is unimportant, and the ball is thrown in a slight arc.

Running
The Principles

Kids love to run. In some ways, running is the easiest skill to teach. Tell your players to run fast and straight, know where the ball is, stay on base

Drill your players to make an L with their throwing arm.

Seven Throwing Tips from Coach Tom McClure

Hold the ball between the fingers and thumb, not in the palm of the hand.

Stare with both eyes; never lose sight of your target.

Point your glove at the target.

Reach back as if you were picking the ball off a table behind you.

Stride and point toes toward the target.

Throw by making an L with your elbow up.

Flip wrist and fingers, pushing down on the ball, for extra speed.

Tom McClure, Northside Youth Organization, Atlanta, Georgia

until the ball is hit, listen to the coaches, and avoid bumping into other play-ers. Have fun!

Baserunning

Players should run on the balls (front section) of their feet with toes pointed straight ahead. They should pump (swing) their arms back and forth with the hands open, not clenched, and the arms bent. Eyes look forward, not down. After the ball is hit, right-handed batters run behind the tee toward first base; left-handed batters run directly toward the base. The batters, now runners, should look at first base, not where the ball has gone. If there's a foul line marked on the field, runners should stay outside of it. Inside the line belongs to the defense. Teach runners to step on and run straight past

After dropping the bat near the tee, this hitter displays near-perfect running form.

Kids love to slide, even when it's not necessary. As coach, you need to be sure they learn how to do it safely, correctly, and effectively. This player should tuck his bent leg under the extended one, keep both arms up, and have his back flat on the ground.

first base without jumping on it or slowing down. The first-base coach is responsible for telling the runner what do next—whether to stay on first base or to continue to second base. Tell your players to listen only to their coach for instructions, not the crowd. When runners are on base, they must keep one foot touching the base until the next batter hits the ball. Base runners should lean forward, watch where the ball goes, and follow the instructions of the nearest coach. Be sure they know not to run past second or third base unless waved ahead by a coach. When passing a base, runners should try to step on its edge without stopping. Runners should never pass a teammate on the base path.

Sliding

Some players will slide into a base at every opportunity, so they must be taught when to slide and how to do it safely for themselves and the defensive players. Sliding is not recommended for the youngest and beginning players.

The runner should start to slide about 4 or 5 feet from the base. Arms are up, fingers are bent, and the chin is down. The runner bends one leg under the other. The lower leg hits the ground first, then the butt, and then the back. The top leg (the extended one) touches the base. The runner should be almost flat on the ground before reaching the base. Headfirst sliding has no place in tee ball.

There are three times to slide: to escape being tagged out, to stop at—not beyond—a base, and to avoid running into another player. Many youngsters have their own reason: sliding is a great attention-getter, especially when crossing home plate. Expect to see it; your responsibility is to see that the slide is done correctly and safely for all involved in the play.

The Practice

Your relationship with your players will be initially formed at the practice sessions. There's more opportunity for one-on-one and small-group instruction at the practices; you'll always be on the field with your team, and you can communicate directly with each child. The players, individually and as a team, will quickly form an opinion of you, so a poor start will be hard to overcome. The practice is the time you (and any assistants) have to help the kids acquire skills by repeated performance of specific actions. Also, there are fewer distractions during practice: no game-time atmosphere, no opposing team, and only a few spectators.

Note: Practice sessions don't always have to be held on a traditional youth baseball or softball field. If facility scheduling is a problem, practices can be held in open, flat, grassy park settings. Bases can be thrown down at their correct locations; if possible, foul lines can be marked off.

A coach, assistant, or parent can easily mark lines on an open field for a tee ball practice or game. T•BALL USA

Preparation

Plan ahead: Well-structured practices are the key to a successful season. Come to each practice with a list of the skills you want to teach or review that day, and allocate a specific amount of time for each element. Decide in advance how to divide the team into smaller groups for more personal instruction and less waiting in line. Plan to be on the field working with each group and each player. Given the age and attention level of your players, plan short drills with many repetitions. Every child should be doing something at all times during the practice session; there should be no standing around watching the other players.

Start with the easier skills (such as throwing) and move on to the more demanding (such as catching fly balls). End the practice with a fun activity that involves the entire team (such as a timed race around the bases). Expect the unexpected!

Prepractice

Before you start your practice, verify that your assistants know where to go and when to be there. Be sure that any nongame functions promised by volunteers (car pools, refreshments, etc.) are taken care of. You must arrive early. Check out the field for the proper placement of the bases and general safety elements. Set out the necessary equipment (e.g., multiple batting tees for three or four groups to use at the same time, some extra gloves). Allow time to talk to parents with questions or concerns. Review the schedule with your assistants or volunteers and give them copies of the day's planned activities. Always start the practice on time. Early arrivals can throw and catch. Latecomers will catch up, and parents will learn to be prompt.

Practice Format

To assist you, a sample tee ball practice session is outlined below. A practice worksheet, like those shown on pages 52 and 53, is an excellent planning tool. Suggested times may be shortened or lengthened depending on such variables as age levels, the learning periods required, the need to concentrate on specific drills, the stage of the season, weather and field conditions, and special requests. If your team consists of younger children (4- and 5-year-olds), the active practice elements (the warm-up and drills) should be kept to about 45 minutes. In most cases, those players 6 years and older will benefit from a 60-minute workout.

- Team meeting: 5 minutes (first meeting will take longer)
- Warm-up: 5 minutes
- Throwing and catching: 10 minutes
- Fielding: 10 minutes

- Defense: 10 minutes
- Running: 5 minutes
- Batting: 20+ minutes
- Closing meeting: 5 minutes
- Snacks and socialization: 15 minutes

An informal game simulation can be held following the active practice elements (see pages 64–65).

Team Meeting (5 minutes)

You may have met some of the players at your preseason meeting (page 29), but at the first practice reintroduce yourself and the assistant coaches and tell the players what tee ball coaches do. Have the players form a circle and call out their names (name tags are a good idea for the first few practices). It's important that you quickly learn every name to accelerate your relationship with the individual players. Explain the basic rules of the game and demonstrate the batting tee. Outline what will happen at practices, and what skills players will be taught. Review the playing field and positions. Learn if any kids on the team have played tee ball before. Try to identify any problems or special situations as early as you can. Be enthusiastic. Smile! Emphasize that tee ball is a fun and active game. If it's not already determined, agree on a team name. End with a cheer: "Let's go, [team name]!" Start the first practice, which should be a short one covering only the basics. Separating the players into small groups will allow you to better evaluate individual skill levels and attitudes about playing a team sport.

All practices should start on time. Tell the team what's planned for the day, what skills you'll work on, and what's expected from the players. At the first practice after a game, go over some of the highlights of that game. Include any amusing things that happened. Remember, tee ball is meant to be fun. Ask for questions. End the meeting with a team cheer.

Tips for the First Meeting from Coach Tom McClure

You must use your judgment as to how much information your kids can process in one practice. Start out with one thing at a time and gradually build up as they fully understand what you have already done. Kids learn at different paces. Be patient! The very first thing you *must* do is draw a baseball field and show your kids all the positions. They will soon be able to point to any position you call out within a few seconds. You must also teach them the objective of the game. Tell them how they should run to first base, then second and third, and then to home plate, and, if you keep score in your league, how a run counts only if they have safely rounded all the bases. Go over elementary defensive strategy. For example, "You are playing third base, and there are runners on first and third base. What do you do if a ground ball is hit to you or a ball is hit in the air?" You will be surprised how fast they pick up the fundamentals, even the concept of double and triple plays.

Tom McClure, Northside Youth Organization, Atlanta, Georgia

Warm-Up (5 minutes)

Youngsters are not as limber as generally believed, and need stretching and warming up of muscles similar to that required by older athletes and adults. Although they have little patience for this activity and want to get on with the sport, recommended prepractice exercises should include stretching (stand straight, touch toes without bending knees, hold in down position, stand up), arm swinging (rotate side to side), running (in place or between bases), playing catch (underhand and overhand throws), and jumping jacks (stand straight, clap hands above the head while jumping in the air, legs split wide apart sideways, jump back to starting position).

Throwing and Catching (10 minutes)

Throwing a ball is a natural movement for kids; they've been doing it since infancy. In standard tee ball, there's no pitching done by the players. They only need to be shown how to develop a good throw, one easily caught by another player. Repetition builds skill, accuracy, and confidence.

Catching requires more instruction, as the technique is different if the ball arrives above or below waist level. Pair off the players and schedule throwing and catching at every practice.

Fielding (10 minutes)

Good fielding requires mastering a mix of fundamental actions, including the proper body and hand positions for ground balls and fly balls, watching the ball go into the glove by trapping or catching it, and always covering the ball. Don't attempt to teach all of the needed skills at once. Give the players time to absorb and master them over an extended period. Start with the basic moves needed to stop a moving ball and add the refinements as the season progresses.

Defense (10 minutes)

Show your players what to do as individuals and as a team when they are in the field, such as where to stand and what happens when they get the ball. Create some gamelike situations, such as an opposing player is on first base or running from third base to home plate. What should they do? Unlike offensive play, defense is where teamwork really counts. Frequently rotate the players around the field positions.

At every practice, tell the team, "Don't crowd around the ball. Play your position."

Running (5 minutes)

Although running comes naturally to kids, baserunning is a skill to be learned. Form, leg strength, and speed can be improved with practice. Good running directly affects the flow of the game. On defense, you'll see a lot of running around in the field after the ball is hit. Effective players must be

mobile; encourage your team to hustle, even when running on and off the playing field.

Batting (20+ minutes)

Hitting is the most important part of tee ball. It's the part of the game that kids anticipate the most, and it often generates the most apprehension and frustration. Hitting becomes the principal measure of success by teammates, parents, and all involved with the sport. Baseball and softball are named for other elements; standard tee ball is focused on hitting a ball off a batting tee. Your players will want to spend as much time at bat as they can. You can speed up the process and maximize individual batting practice turns by setting up small groups at additional batting locations in the outfield. With a coach or assistant coach supervising, one player hits and the other participants field and return the balls. Make sure the layout ensures safety to the nearby batting stations. Good team hitting will be an important measure of your accomplishments as a coach. Keep it fun. Remember there's a unique combination of physical and mental forces at work within your young players. Practice. Practice. Practice.

Left: This player shows good form in getting his body and the fingers on both hands down to field an oncoming ground ball.

Right: A typical fielding situation. Drill your players to stay in their assigned positions.

Practice Session Worksheet

Team meeting (5 min.):

_____

_____

_____

Warm-up (5 min.):

_____

_____

_____

Throwing and catching (10 min.):

_____

_____

_____

Fielding (10 min.):

_____

_____

_____

Defense (10 min.):

_____

_____

_____

Running (5 min.):

_____

_____

_____

Batting (20+ min.):

_____

_____

Closing meeting (5 min.):

_____

_____

_____

Snacks and socialization (15 min.):

_____

_____

Practice Session Worksheet

Team meeting (5 min.):
First full practice—check out uniforms and equipment
Explain today's program
Answer any questions

Warm-up (5 min.):
Stretching
Jumping jacks
Run to first base

Throwing and catching (10 min.):
Demonstrate the grip
Show correct body position
Practice overhand throws to a coach

Fielding (10 min.):
How to stand for ground balls
Glove position
Catch ball and cover with other hand

Defense (10 min.):
Roll or hit balls to team

Running (5 min.):
Practice running to first base

Batting (20+ min.):
Have every player hit from batting tee set on
home plate

Closing meeting (5 min.):
Praise team for hard work and effort
Show one drill to do at home
End with team cheer

Snacks and socialization (15 min.):
Time for refreshments and conversation!

Advice for New Coaches

The most important thing to keep in mind is to make tee ball fun for everyone (including yourself). Think of creative ways of introducing and practicing skills. Acknowledge kids when they get it right. Help kids work on the skills they need to improve upon individually—at practices, not during games in front of a crowd. Think of the joy you can give a group of kids for just a small amount of your time and energy. I still run into kids from several years past who recognize me as "Coach."

Reed Davis, Youth Sports Director, South Suburban Parks and Recreation, Fullerton, Colorado

Closing Meeting (5 minutes)

Point out all the good things the team did together during the practice. Compliment them on their hard work. Be specific: identify individual players who quickly learned a new skill or improved their overall practice performance. Give the team one skill to practice or one drill to do at home. Ask for a show of hands to see who will practice at home until the next time the team meets. End the meeting with a team cheer and let the players run to be with their families.

Snacks and Socialization (15 minutes)

Postpractice snack time serves two purposes. The kids need some refreshment, especially fluids, and they need time to talk with each other, parents, and friends. You'll learn a lot from discreetly monitoring their conversa-

Bob Costas on Tee Ball

Tee ball is a great introduction to baseball or softball. It's fun, unthreatening, and almost always inadvertently humorous. I played tee ball more than forty years ago. I can't remember all my stats, but I can tell you this—I never struck out.

Bob Costas, NBC Sports

tions—what they like and the things that bother them. It's good to have a preview, as some of these matters may soon come back to you from their parents. Snack time is best held near the practice field so that the group can stay together and not quickly break up and disperse.

Questions and Answers

Q. Some players say they don't remember the rules. What can I do about this?

A. Parents can help; make sure they understand the basic rules and regulations. See the rules sidebars for kids and parents on pages 26 and 27.

Q. What happens when a player misses a practice?

A. First, it's important to find out why. Was there a schedule conflict? Perhaps there was a doctor's appointment, school activity, illness, or did the parents simply forget? It may be that the child didn't want to go to practice. When you learn the reason, you'll be better able to handle the situation. As your practice sessions will contain many repetitions of the basic skills, an interested player will quickly catch up. If a large number of kids couldn't attend, begin your next practice with a review of any new skills taught at the previous session.

Q. If, for some unexpected reason, I can't be at the practice, should I cancel it?

A. No. Always be sure your assistants know what you plan to cover that day. They can follow the worksheet you prepared. Or they can change the practice to a review of skills previously introduced and have players do some of the fun-oriented drills that they like best.

Sample Practices

This chapter describes two sample practices, one for the younger, beginning players and one for the older, more experienced participants. It also details a simulated game format. At either level, it's important that you, as coach, be able to talk to every kid individually during the practice session. Use their first name or nickname. Make eye contact. Be constructive and encouraging. Remind each player that he or she is important to the team.

You may want to split the children into beginner and advanced sections at the first few practices. Once the first-time players have gained an understanding of the fundamentals, combine the two groups and run the drills that the kids can accomplish together. They are a team.

Make notes of the players' development. Some kids do well and quickly master skills; others may need more repetition of the basics. You can modify drills to produce specific results. As the team progresses and gains experience and confidence, you can replace the drills in the sample practices with different drills from chapters 9, 10, and 11. Variety will enhance the kids' attention and make the practices less routine and more fun.

Basic Beginning Practice

This practice is primarily designed for the youngest and least skilled players who are just starting to learn how to play tee ball. It covers the fundamental techniques for throwing, catching, fielding, hitting, running, and the positioning of players on the field. Select the drills based on the progress that individuals and the group are making. Select drills for 45 minutes of active practice. (Remember that several drills can be run simultaneously in different areas.) The total session, including meetings and snack time, should last about an hour.

Team Meeting

At the first meeting, you should walk the team around the field and show the players each position. Let them stand at each position for a moment, and

Coaching Tip

When talking to players, kneel down so that your eyes are level with theirs. Parents, if standing or sitting, often look down at their children when giving instructions. You will be a more effective coach if you can communicate face-to-face with the youngsters.

call out the name of each position. Explain the main objective of the game: to hit the ball and run safely to first base and then—usually with the help of their teammates—try to get to second, third, and back to home plate. Advise them that when they are the defense (playing out in the field) they should think about what to do if the ball comes in their direction. Every practice should begin with you telling the players what they will be doing that day and reminding them to have fun.

Warm-Up

The first on-field activity is a short warm-up (see page 50.) Stretching and running are the most important activites to do at this time.

Throwing

- **Show Me** and **Use the L.** These two drills should be part of every practice session to be sure that the players are holding the ball correctly and standing with their throwing arm in the proper position.   **W1**   **W2**

- **One-Knee Throws.** This drill forces the players to concentrate on their arm and upper-body movement, as it eliminates leg action.   **W3**

Catching

- **Catch.** There's no defense in tee ball until all the players can catch the ball. This drill can also be done away from the practice field and should be assigned as homework to do with parents, siblings, or friends.   **W7**

Call out "L!" before the fielder throws the ball.

- **Catching Flies.** Some children need to overcome the fear of being hit by a ball coming down on them from above. All players need to practice catching fly balls correctly and safely. W9

Throwing and Catching

- **One and Two.** This game builds two skills in a minimally competitive format. W10

- **Back and Forth.** This popular drill is used at all levels of baseball and softball. Start with a distance of less than 20 feet between the throwers and catchers; increase the distance as these two basic skills are mastered. W11

Fielding

- **Crab Drill.** This is an excellent introduction to basic defense and should be part of every practice session. W15

- **Scoop or Pickup.** The object of this drill is to practice the trapping of rolling or bouncing balls. W16

- **Mini-Pepper.** This indispensable fielding drill can be used at all levels of baseball. W17

- **Just Block It.** Use this activity as a drill or a game to teach players to stop a batted ball before it goes through the infield and ends up in the outfield. W20

- **Bare Hand.** Fielders need to practice picking up a nonmoving ball with their open (ungloved) hand. W21

Defense

- **First Base–Third Base.** This drill involves the entire team working simulta-neously in two groups. The action is designed to improve defensive play-ing skills. **D1**

- **Fastest Fingers.** Speed, coordination, and agility are rewarded in this popu-lar defense-based game. **D3**

Running

- **Who's on First?** This drill will give you an excellent opportunity to see the running form and speed of each player on the team. **W27**

- **What Now?** Players must learn to listen to their first-base coach for what to do after they safely reach the base. This drill condi-tions them to be alert for instructions and then to follow them. **W28**

Record the players' running times to first base; as the season progresses, you'll be able to see how their times improve.

- **Catch the Team.** Here's an excellent event to end a practice session with the entire team running off the field together. **W33**

Batting

- **Invisible Bat.** This drill appeals to players of all ages. Demonstrate it at the first batting prac-tice. No equipment is needed; suggest that kids can practice this on their own, any-where there's a little room to swing their arms. **B1**

- **Tee Time.** This is the most effective drill to develop batting skill. Schedule for every batting practice. **B3**

- **Coach Says.** Players enjoy this fast-paced routine. Delegate a parent to run the drill while you're working with individual players, who can leave and reenter the drill. **B5**

Closing Meeting

Review the day's accomplishments. Assign a drill to practice at home (see page 54).

Snacks and Socialization

This is the time for refreshments and conversation (see pages 31 and 54–55).

Advanced Practice

These drills require some understanding of and ability to perform the fundamental skills required to play tee ball. Feel free to repeat or modify drills from the basic beginning practice as a refresher for the more experienced players. Select drills for 60 minutes of active practice. (Remember several drills can be run simultaneously in different areas.) The total session, including meetings and snack time, should last about 80 minutes.

Team Meeting

Inform the team what they will be doing and why. Ask and answer questions about practice.

Warm-Up

Begin the practice with exercises (see page 50). Include jumping jacks and, time permitting, a run around the bases.

Throwing

- **Crow-Hop.** Here's a drill that helps develop the players' throwing skills and lets them look and feel more experienced. **W6**

- **Bounce to the Bucket.** Run this practice as a game that rewards accuracy. **W4**

- **One-Knee Throws.** Modify the basic maneuver (**W3**) by beginning with 15 feet between the partners and gradually increasing the distance to 25 feet (half the distance between the bases).

Catching

- **Catching Flies.** At this level, all balls should be hit in the air from the batting tee by a coach or adult volunteer. Use a soft practice tee ball. **W9**

Throwing and Catching

- **Diamond Drill.** Upgrade the basic routine (W13) by hitting or rolling the ball to the player in the pitching area.

- **Moving Target.** For maximum skill development, the receiver must be instructed to change location for each throw. W14

Fielding

- **The Triangle.** This drill improves sideways movement, agility, and footwork. W22

- **Distraction.** There is often a crowd of defensive players running to reach ground balls. This drill is designed to keep a fielder focused on an incoming ball. W18

- **Dive.** Just as in baseball and softball, hustle helps. Have the fielders practice safely diving for the ball; remind them that headfirst sliding is not allowed. W19

Kids will dive for the ball, especially if other fielders are trying to get there first. Try to minimize crowding and emphasize safety.

- **Reverse.** The advanced players should be able to catch balls hit or thrown over their heads and behind them. **W23**

- **Fun-Go.** A simulated inning of defense is an excellent way to end fielding practice. **D7**

Catchers' Drills

- **Go Get.** The catcher needs to practice safely fielding a fair ball hit to the infield, which can become an area crowded with defensive players. **W25**

- **Protect the Plate.** Base runners attempting to cross home plate have two safety concerns: colliding with the catcher and bumping into the batting tee. This drill will teach the catcher where to stand. The offensive coach or another adult must always remove the tee after a ball is put into play. **W26**

Defense

- **Dee-Fense.** All fielders must be ready and able to get base runners out; this drill helps build the necessary skills. **D6**

- **Pizza Slices.** This drill takes time to set up and explain, but it's a proven way to establish player position strategy. Kids quickly grasp and remember that they should stay in or near their designated area. **D8**

Running

- **Track Meet.** This drill allows you to evaluate the form and speed of the players and correct any flaws in running technique. **W30**

- **Catch the Coach.** This drill helps establish the personal relationship between you and the players. There's a lot of running involved, so you can limit the game to two or three kids at each practice and let the rest of the team cheer for their teammates. **W31**

Batting

- **Tee Time.** This is the one essential batting practice drill for all levels of play. **B3**

- **Numbers.** Created for the more experienced players, the drill also includes some fielding practice. **B4**

Closing Meeting

Review the day's accomplishments and areas for improvement. Demonstrate a drill to be practiced at home (see page 54).

Snacks and Socialization

This is the time for refreshments and conversation (see pages 31 and 54–55).

Practicing Field Positions

Players need to know where to stand on the field. As rotation is an important part of the learning cycle and game play action, every player on the team must be familiar with each defensive position (see pages 13–14 for details). The position information outlined below is the same for both sample practices. The participants in the basic beginning workout need repetitions of the fundamentals. The more complex drills (tagging base runners, multiple ball relays, the crow-hop) can be reserved for the advanced practice players. The speed and reaction times for the fielding drills at each position can be accelerated at both levels as the season progresses. The coach and assistant coaches initiate and direct play action.

First base. Show where the first-base player should be when no base runner is on base (stands in fair territory away from the base) and when a runner is on the base (stands in fair territory next to the base). The player practices fielding plays, such as tagging or forcing a runner out.

Second base. Position a player at second base, showing the proper defensive position. The player practices fielding plays, such as tagging or forcing a runner out.

Third base. Position a player at third base, showing the proper defensive location. The player practices fielding ground balls, stepping on the base, and throwing to home plate.

Shortstop. Position a player as shortstop. The player practices fielding balls and throwing to first or second base for an out. At least once, have the player throw to third base.

Right infielder, left infielder. Players can get practice in the infield by following the same practice as the shortstop.

"Pitcher." In tee ball, the pitcher acts as an

This is good defensive form.

infielder. Position a player as pitcher, who practices fielding the ball and throwing to first base and to the catcher.

Catcher. After the ball is hit by a coach, an adult removes the tee and bat, and the catcher moves up to cover home plate. The player practices tagging a base runner out, fielding the ball, and throwing to first base.

General infield activity. Players must stay behind the playing line until the ball is hit. Players practice catching short fly balls, fielding ground balls and throwing to a base or home plate, tagging a runner on the base path, and relaying a ball from an outfielder to the catcher.

Outfielders. There may be as many as seven. Show each player what area to cover. Players practice catching fly balls in a crowd, and trapping ground balls and throwing to an infielder. Have one outfielder receive a ball relayed from another outfielder and throw it to an infielder.

Game Simulation

Once the basic tee ball skills have been acquired by the players to some degree of competence, a gamelike format can be added to the practice session. A basic beginning group may require more time spent on the fundamentals before trying to put them into an actual game situation. An advanced team should be able to perform in a simulated game earlier in the pregame period.

Practice Game

The entire team takes the field on defense except for the catcher, who becomes the first batter. If an out is made, the batter goes to right field and the team rotates positions. The pitcher becomes the next batter, the first-base player moves to the pitching area, the second-base player to first base, the third-base player to shortstop, the left fielder to third base, and so on through all of the positions. If the batter successfully gets on base, the rotation is the same, except no one goes to right field. If there are only nine players on the team and the batters are getting on base, the outfield may become depleted;

What I Like about My Coach

My coach teaches me the right way to do things. I learned how to run, field, and bat. We have fun learning how to play baseball. The coaches teach kids at their own level. Some kids need extra help in batting or fielding so the coach teaches them what they need.

When I field the ball and throw, the coach is trying to get me to throw more overhand instead of sidearm. He says I throw sidearm, but I think I throw better if it's a little sidearm.

I like the coach because he makes sure that everybody gets a turn to bat and a turn to play in the field. He also teaches us games, like running the bases, races, and catching games. I really liked the running race. Two kids start at home plate and launch off and run the bases in opposite directions. They pass each other near second base and meet at the finish back at home plate. The first one to get there wins. That was fun!

Eric Jaspersen, 6 years old, Bedford–Pound Ridge Little League, Bedford, New York

---

Rotation System for Skills Training

Divide the team up into three groups. Team A bats, team B plays the right side of the field (pitcher, first base, second base, right field, and any other defensive players positioned on the right), and team C plays the left side of the field (catcher, shortstop, third base, left field, and any other players positioned on the left). The center fielder can be set either slightly to the right with team B or to the left with team C.

Each player on team A bats three times (there is no baserunning), and then the entire group rotates to the right side of the field. Team B rotates to the left side. The players who had been playing in the outfield switch to infield positions, and the players from the infield move to the outfield. Team C bats. Then rotate again: team A goes to the left area, team B comes to bat, and team C moves to the right side of the field. This procedure allows each child to hit three times and play two defensive positions within a short period. More importantly, it keeps the players' attention because they are constantly moving.

The drill is effective because it covers three elements of the game: hitting, infield, and outfield play. It builds to a total basic understanding of tee ball and prepares the team for the next steps in their development.

Richard Blalock, Diamond Sports Park, Gainesville, Florida

have parent volunteers fill the empty spaces. Assistant coaches are positioned on the field to advise the runners and oversee the players' rotation. Players who are put out after getting on base or who safely round the bases reenter the game in the outfield.

The coach works at home plate adjusting the tee, placing the ball on the tee, advising the batters, and covering the plate defensively.

A variation with advanced players is to have the pitcher come in to cover home plate after the ball is hit past the playing line when there are base runners on second or third base. The practice game is over after every player has been at bat one time and has played at every defensive position. It should be completed in about 30 minutes, depending on the number of players available. If field availability or other scheduling conflicts don't allow time for a simulation game, eliminate some of the drills or reduce the time allotted for regular practice segments.

"Spring Training"

Try to arrange a one-inning practice game with another team in your league. Each team bats and plays in the field, rotating defensive positions with each opposing batter. Your kids will be excited, enjoy the semicompetitive atmosphere, and have fun really playing together as a team.

Checklist

A checklist of things for a coach to do on and off the field is located in the appendix.

CHAPTER 7

Game Time

The Mental Aspect

It's the first game of the season. The kids are excited. For many, it's the first time they've played on a team in an (even minimally) competitive situation. They know that parents, siblings, other family members, and friends will be there to watch them play. Some may not realize that another group of spectators will be at the game to cheer the other team. No one expects perfection from the kids, but your coaching abilities and your interactions with the children will be closely observed and discussed. There may not be winners and losers in your league, but, as coach, you can always score high marks. How? By good planning, an optimistic approach to the event, and conveying enthusiasm and support for every player. In all phases of game day—before, during, and after—remember the opportunity you have to influence kids and help their families, your community, and yourself.

Set an Example

If you've taught the players to pay attention to you and the other coaches during the game, they probably will (but not always). However, they can't demonstrate good sportsmanship or fair play if you display any inappropriate actions, physical or verbal. Contain your emotions. Treat the umpires with respect; they may be parents or teenagers. Sometimes there are bad or questionable calls. Accept them. Don't become involved with the players of the opposing team; they have their own coach. Be spirited and vocal, but always polite and mannerly. Your actions will be more influential to the team than any lectures you may have given them about behavior on and off the field.

Look the Part

If your league has a dress code for coaches, follow it. Otherwise, meet with the other coaches in your league and agree upon a similar appearance. A favored look is khaki pants or shorts and a collared sport shirt that matches the colors of the team's uniforms. Many leagues order adult sizes of the team's T-shirts for the coaches. The important point is to look neat, authoritative, and part of the team.

Know the Rules

There are variations in the rules for tee ball play around the country. Many leagues strictly follow the regulations directed by their national or regional youth baseball organizations. A growing number of leagues (usually non-aligned and independent) modify the rules to adapt to community requests. Be sure to understand the rules that apply where your team plays. It's a good idea to have a copy of your league's rules with you.

Before the Game

Be Prepared

Have your batting order (distribute the more skilled batters throughout the batting order) and starting field positions ready. Plan any rotations. Be flexible about making changes, as some players may arrive late. Also, parents sometimes forget to call about their child not being able to come to the game. Prior to the game, contact the persons responsible for transportation and refreshments to be sure that all necessary arrangements have been made. Call your assistants and volunteers to verify their participation. Plan to arrive 45 minutes or more before game time; you need to be there before the players arrive. Check out the equipment and the condition of the field in terms of safety.

Meet the Other Coaches and Umpires

Establish personal relationships. You'll probably be on the field with them again during the season. Confirm that both teams are playing under the same rules. If not, resolve any differences and inform your assistants, players, and parents of any modifications. Learn if the umpire has to make any changes due to the condition of the playing field.

Warm-Up

Time permitting, have players do 5 minutes of stretching, a few minutes of running, and then 10 minutes of throwing and catching with their coaches,

USA Baseball and Tee Ball

Successful baseball players at all levels possess a common trait: sound fundamentals. In our national pastime, tee ball serves a critical role in establishing the sound fundamentals all players need, at every level. Additionally, tee ball may teach players the greatest lesson of all—that baseball is fun.

Paul V. Seiler, Executive Director and CEO, USA Baseball

parents, or volunteers (the experienced players can do this warm-up element with each other).

Pep Talk

Ask who practiced at home. Talk to the players about paying attention and doing their best. Remind them to stand in the proper fielding position before the batter hits, to think about what to do if the ball is hit to them, to always know where the ball is, and if any runners are on base. Give them a specific goal for the day, such as staying in position and not all converging on the ball. Ask them to be sure to call "I've got it!" when fielding a ball. Sit the team on the bench in batting order, with the first batter seated closest to home plate. Assign their defensive positions. Remind them to have fun, and end the meeting with the team cheer.

Tell your players that they are a team and must all work together. Encourage them to help one another play well and to have a good time.

Coaching the Game

The Start of the Game

If your team begins on offense, have the first batter put on a safety helmet and take a few warm-up swings (see **B2**) in an area at a distance from other players or spectators. When the umpire calls "Play ball!" the player goes to home plate and assumes the batting stance. Kneel across from the batter, adjust the tee to the correct height, and place the ball on the tee. Give a short message of motivation, back away, and let the game begin. The next player to bat can take warm-up swings during this interval. Everyone on the bench slides over toward home plate. The cycle is repeated for each player during the inning.

If your team begins the game on defense, have the players run out to their positions and be ready to play.

During the Game: On Defense

Many leagues allow—and even encourage—parents to be on the field with their children's team; check your league's rules. If permitted, one parent is stationed between first and second base, one between second and third base, and often two in the outfield. Remind players to go back to their original positions after every play. Defensive coaches working with the on-field parents should tell the players what to do if they get the ball. If the fielding is below your expectations and creating frustration for the players, instruct them (during a break in the action or between innings) to always watch the ball go into the glove and to use both hands when catching it. The ball should be returned to the offensive coach at home plate unless the play has ended there.

During the Game: On Offense

When your team is on the bench before batting, quickly review any situation that may have occurred when they were in the field. Be sure that coaches or assistants are stationed at first and third base to give instructions to the base runners. A parent should also be at these bases to assist coaches in giving instructions, encouraging players, checking that runners are wearing safety helmets, and with crowd control, retrieving balls, and other tasks. If allowed, have a coach or parent at second base to direct base runner traffic. Remind runners to listen to the base coaches and to stand facing the tee with their left foot touching the base. When coaching the players at bat, remind them to set down the bat, not to throw it. Move the dropped bat away from home plate, especially when there are base runners.

Chatter

During games, encourage both teams. Calling out "Good hustle!," "Nice try!," and "Great!" will have short- and long-term benefits for the individual

Native American Tee Ball

The Friendship Youth Sports League is an organization made up of different Native American Tribes all getting together to play in a noncompetitive sports league that stresses participation, skill development, good sportsmanship, and friendly games. The league plays many different sports, but tee ball is the most popular. It draws overflowing crowds whenever the teams get together. Many different tribes play in the tee ball league, including the Fort McDowell Yavapai Indian Nation, Salt River, Ak-Chin, Sacaton, Gila River, Guadalupe Yaquis, and the Laveen. On game night the parks are packed with parents, brothers and sisters, grandparents, aunts, uncles, and cousins. It is not just a game; it's an event. Tee ball brings out everyone from all over the reservation. Many treat this as a social occasion where they revisit friends from other reservations they played sports with in the Old Days.

We don't keep track of winning and losing, so the players can focus on skill development and having lots of fun. What we're trying to do is promote sportsmanship. We say, "Every kid's a winner and every team's a champion." It's easy for us to form tee ball teams on the reservation because many kids have lots of relatives. Some teams are constructed with one family and a few cousins. The great part about tee ball play in the Friendship League is that the players not only cheer for their own team but for the other team. They learn to respect the other side and clap when a good play is made. Sportsmanship is taught to the children at an early age and, hopefully, will carry out with them as they get older. Our kids are the number-one commodity, and we hope to help each one grow into a respectful adult.

Gary Schwartz, Sports Coordinator, Fort McDowell Yavapai Indian Nation Parks and Recreation, near Phoenix, Arizona

players and the teams. The players should be reminded to communicate positive words to their teammates while in the field or from the bench. Hearing "Good try!" from another player after a failed defensive or offensive play can be immeasurably supportive to a child in an early-age sport. Keep your team involved and cheering.

After the Game

Sportsmanship

Have your team line up and high-five the opposing team. Do the team cheer.

Taking Stock

Gather the team for a short meeting. Review good performances. Ask the players to recall one thing they saw a teammate do that was "really cool." Examples include a big hit, a great catch, a safe on base after a fast run, teamwork. Briefly discuss any negative matters, but don't linger on them. Your philosophy should be that "mistakes teach us what not to do," and then you work to correct these mistakes at the next practice. Give players a drill to do at home (see chapter 12). Finally, have the kids join their parents for snack time refreshments. Be available to give parents an opportunity to talk with you. Expect some criticism. There are no perfect games in tee ball, but every game should be fun to play and watch. Remind players of the date, time, and place of the next game or practice.

Questions and Answers

Q. My team is all 5- and 6-year-olds. How many have to show up in order to play?

A. At that age, ten players make for a good game. Put in a right infielder between first and second base. If you have more than ten, position one or two more in the infield and the rest in the outfield (remember, there's a fifteen-player maximum). Fewer than nine players leads to too many hits, as the fielding suffers.

Q. Our league uses some teenagers as umpires. I'm uncomfortable protesting what I perceive as unfair calls as my players relate so well to these young game officials. What's your advice?

A. If an umpire of any age makes an error in judgment, you should accept the decision. At the end of the half-inning, calmly discuss the call privately with the umpire. Refrain from shouting or any public display of anger. Your objective is to help the umpire and prevent similar future judgments. Keep parents out of the discussion. Demonstrate to your team the same respect and sportsmanship you expect them to exhibit.

Q. After the ball is hit, when is the ball considered dead? What happens to any runners on base?

A. The ball is dead if it doesn't pass the playing line. The batter should run to first base in case the ball becomes fair; if it's dead, the batter goes back to the batting tee. Any base runners return to their base. In terms of game ball play, there is no difference between the dead ball

Comments from a Professional Coach

As I was growing up, I had a good base—a solid foundation—at home. I had Little League coaches, high school coaches, college coaches, professional, and Major League coaches. They gave me the skills I needed on and off the field. I was taught the fundamentals of the game and was provided a value system that enabled me to pursue my lifelong dream of a coaching career and establishing successful sports camps throughout the country.

Before being a player and coach with the New York Mets and the Baltimore Orioles, I participated at every level of baseball. Today, having my own baseball camps enables me to pass on the lessons I learned. Leadership, sportsmanship, cooperation, and respect are as important as winning. I am also able to experience the greatest feeling—the gleam in the eyes of my sons and daughter—as they experience the joys of the game. As a parent coaching tee ball, you will realize many moments of satisfaction and accomplishment as you fulfill your responsibilities to your league, team, family, and child.

Rob Dromerhauser, President, American Sports Academy

Qualities in a Good Coach

First and foremost, to be a good coach you need to be able to relate to children and understand their different learning styles and abilities. A good coach can read a child's emotions and speak to them on their level, with age-appropriate terminology. The most effective way to approach coaching is to ensure the child benefits from the game, finding camaraderie in the team and experiencing the rush of competition. The foundation of our athletic program is sportsmanship: teaching kids how to be good sports, how to co-operate and problem-solve together, how to support one another, and what it means to work as a team to help each other be successful. A good coach is a teacher, teaching a skill that becomes an important part of their moral and ethical formation. Coaching is not a self-regarding fulfillment; it is passing on life skills to our youth, teaching a code of conduct, treating all skill levels equally, and ensuring every child gets playing time. Being a coach means having an understanding of the game, but most importantly, having an understanding of what it takes to fulfill a child's eagerness, determination, and inherent need to be accepted as a teammate.

Tari Irvin, Program Services and Training Director, Boys & Girls Clubs of King County, Seattle, Washington

zone and the foul zone; the dead ball zone includes the foul ball territory in front of home plate.

Q. We had a practice game with a local team from another league. Their coach called outs. My understanding is that there are no outs in tee ball. The other coach also said there are outs when the bases are tagged. What is correct?

A. Outs occur whenever an offensive player cannot safely reach a base. If you're playing bat-around, every player may be called out, but the team's turn at bat isn't over until all the players have been at bat one time. If you're playing that three outs make a (half) inning, then the players switch sides when the third out happens.

Next, there are two definitions of *tag*. A batter or base runner is out when a defensive player tags (steps on) a base before the offensive player gets there or when a fielder holding the ball in a hand or glove tags (touches) a runner with the ball.

Q. Where should coaches be during a game?

A. Two coaches may be on the field for the team at bat and stand in foul territory near first and third base. The defensive team may also have

What I Learned from My Coach

I learned the most important rules to live by from my tee ball coach when I was just 5 years old. They are: Play fair, try hard, and have fun. These rules apply on the playground, in the classroom, and even at home. I'd like to thank my tee ball coach for teaching me these rules . . . and which way to run to first base.

Trey Nelson, 12 years old, San Ramon, California

two coaches on the field in foul territory, but they should be at least 10 feet beyond the first and third bases. All other coaches must be off the field, except in games with very young, beginning players. Coaches are not permitted to run along the baseline or to touch or assist a base runner while the ball is in play. A coach may position a batter at home plate but must move away from the home plate area before the player hits the ball. A fair or live ball that touches a coach (or umpire) on the field remains in play.

Q. How should I respond when a parent of one of my players says, "My son could use some encouragement. He's nervous about playing his first tee ball league game."

A. The parent can tell the child three things: The boy is part of a team, not just out there on his own. Tee ball is about learning baseball skills, but it's mainly to have fun. Tee ball will get him started in baseball and can lead to many years of good times playing or as a fan.

As the kid's coach (and his new authority figure), you should give your player the same advice. Tell the parent to have fun, too; remind him or her that it's only a game.

Dealing with Parents, Gender Issues, and Safety and Health

The relationship between coaches and parents is complex and one of the most important topics in youth sports. It is frequently examined in books and newspaper and magazine articles, and on television and call-in radio shows. There's also substantial content on the topic on the Internet. Parents talk about coaches; coaches talk about parents; kids talk about both. Obviously, there are differences between individual and team sports. A single athlete and a coach have a one-on-one relationship. In some team sports, the coach deals with only a small number of players and parents. You may be involved with as many as twenty kids and their parents. The level of play—from primarily recreational to competitive—is a factor. Players will range from absolute beginners in sports to those with some experience in team play. This chapter centers on the elements that apply in tee ball.

You are both a baffled parent and a rookie coach. You need to deal with other baffled parents and those who have previously participated in tee ball or different youth sports. You have a kid on the team and so do they. Other parents may also be new coaches, experienced coaches, or active volunteers. In this mix, there will be parents who know (or think they know) more about tee ball than you do and other parents totally dependent on you to help them and their child. There will be some parents who, unfortunately, view the tee ball program as a place to park their kid for a few hours.

The Role of the Parents

In many ways, parents are vital to the success of the program. Parents can step forward (as you may have done) to be coaches, assistant coaches, or volunteers, but you must encourage every parent to become involved in their child's tee ball experience. Ask parents if they would like to help. Some may want to but won't offer their services if they see you already have assistance.

Parents may not always communicate their goals, but they usually want their child to participate in a safe sport, learn the rules and the skills,

Maximize your opportunities to talk with the parents, individually and in groups, before and after practices and games.

experience team play, get some exercise, meet other kids, and have fun. Some parents enjoy the opportunity to meet other parents and become involved in the social aspects of a community activity. Try to establish an environment where the parents can actively help the tee ball program and strengthen your position without intruding into your areas of responsibility, authority, and experience.

At Practice

It's important that parents bring their child to practices and games on time. When kids are late, they may miss your team meeting or early drills. Sometimes you'll have to bring kids into the group; they may be shy or embarrassed.

Focusing on the Parents

Our programs through the YMCA are based on volunteer support from the parents. We try to involve the parents as much as possible through coaching, assistant coaching, and team captains. Parent involvement is crucial to making the program a success. The focus of my tee ball program is based more on the aspects of fun and excitement for the kids and parents while instilling interest in fundamentals. If the children are having fun, then the parents are having fun. Clear communication between the parents and coaches and the parents and the organization is key to running a smooth league. Parents love to be informed and kept in the loop on decisions involving their children.

Josh Ransdell, Youth Sports Program Director, Southwest YMCA, Louisville, Kentucky

Parents should participate with their child in learning and developing basic skills and a knowledge of the sport. Establish a time and identify specific drills where parents can come onto the field and work with their child during the practice sessions. This allows parents to interact with their child (and other parents and children) and also develops a basis for working with their child beyond the defined scope of the tee ball program. Before practice, parents can help coaches prepare the field and check it for safety. During practice, they can help by recovering batted or thrown balls and keeping nonparticipants off the field.

Tee ball mom and dad helping their son practice his batting in a local playground.

Pregame

Parents must be sure that their child is dressed properly and has the necessary equipment (basically, a glove and a marked water bottle). The players' enthusiasm is welcome before a game, but kids who are running around are wasting their energy. The parents should maintain control until the team is fully assembled for the team meeting. Parents should show their child where they will be during the game.

During Games

Parents can help on the field and as base coaches. Off the field, parents, other family members, and friends can provide support via cheers and encouragement. If a child is making a real effort, hearing "Nice try!" from a parent is meaningful. Parents should root for all the players and the team by its name.

A tee ball dad helps his daughter on the field.

Postgame

This is the time when the players reunite with their parents. It's not a time for either you or the parents to dwell on any negatives that occurred during the game. Remind the parents to congratulate all the players. The kids will

---

Can the Coaching Parent Leave the Game at the Field?

One of the hardest lessons for a parent who decides to coach his or her child's team for the first time is to leave what happens in a game or practice at the diamond. Too often the parent-coach will continue to discuss some aspect of the child's performance—usually a negative aspect—long after the game has ended. I've seen these discussions extend well into the evening following the event and sometimes even continue for days. The last thing your child wants is to be reminded of the hit not made in a key situation or the missed defensive play. The coaching parent needs to remember that these are kids *playing a game*; above all, it needs to be a positive and rewarding experience for them. As much as parents may want to relive their own youth or athletic career through their child, each youngster deserves his or her own special time. Not all kids grow up to be Barry Bonds or Derek Jeter. Most will grow up and get a normal job, and their only sports experience might be some form of organized sports as a young child. With this in mind, the coaching parent needs to be sure not to transfer other problems at home to the child's performance in the sport. Be positive and remember, in the end, it's only a game. That dropped ball or ground out or bad throw has very little to do with your child's enjoyment of tee ball. The most important thing to kids is that you tell them they did a good job and that you are proud of them.

On a personal note, I have found in my 10 years of coaching that although to some players winning and losing is everything, to most kids the most important part of the game is . . . what's for snacks?

Roy Nelson, President, Canyon Creek Little League, San Ramon, California

---

be thinking about snack time, and the parents should be prepared to hand out the food and beverages. Parents should assist in putting away all the equipment—balls, bats, bases, safety helmets, etc.

At Home

Parents must give time and attention to working on players' basic skill development (see chapter 12 for details). As appropriate, parents should involve siblings in positive conversations about the family's tee ball experience, and brothers and sisters can participate in certain fielding and running drills. Remind the parents to tell their child that their family and school are more important than tee ball or any other activity. The older players must first help around the house and do their homework before they even think about practicing.

Communication

You need to get to know the parents as well as your players. Name tags for parents are a good idea for the first few practices. Distribute information about the game and the program (see the sample letter in chapter 3 and the rules sidebar in chapter 2). Consider a midseason newsletter about the team's progress. Have a parent or teenager set up a Web page to post schedule data, news, and pictures of the team. Feedback from the parents will influence your performance. Try to talk with them informally—individually or in small groups—but away from your players. A phone call can clear up or

There is nothing better than a big hug to express a parent's pride in their child's tee ball participation.

Parental Code of Conduct

- Exhibit exceptionally good social behavior at practice sessions and games or stay away from these activities.
- See that your children—the players—have the proper equipment.
- See that your children arrive at the stated time and are picked up at the stated time.
- Applaud all good efforts and good plays or remain silent.
- Allow the coaches to coach without outside interference or influence.
- See that your children receive ample positive encouragement and hugs regardless of the outcome of their games.
- Allow your children to play without negative pressure, verbal or physical.
- Support the coaches in what they want the players to learn.
- Treat the coaches, league leaders, and game umpires with dignity and respect.
- See that your children do not intentionally injure other players.

Jack Hutslar, Ph.D., CEO, North American Youth Sports Institute

minimize misunderstandings. Remember, you have the dual role of coach and parent. This should enable you to anticipate parental problems and concerns.

Winning

If your league keeps score and has winning and losing as part of its program, it's important to understand the parents' point of view on this matter. Yes, competition is the essence of sports. Parents will want their kids' team to win, but they need to understand that there are more important goals to work toward, including using the new skills, playing different positions, teamwork, and having fun. Even the youngest children are exposed to winning and losing. They see it in other sports and social games, on TV, and at

Successful Tee Ball Coaches' Tips for Dealing with Parents

- The children with the best attitudes improve the most, and parents are the principal influence on the kids' feelings about the sport.

- Parents need to realize that most kids want to play for themselves instead of for the parent.

- Establish reasonable expectations; don't set unrealistic goals for the kids, the team, or the parents.

- Remind the parents that they are not playing—tee ball is a game for young children.

- As coach, you're important to every child. Be supportive and encouraging to them. A good relationship with the parents will ensure their help and confidence to do the job you volunteered to do.

- The best thing parents can do is learn how to coach their own children. Every kid can learn to hit the ball. Parents need to work with their children. Throwing and catching a ball is fun. Tell the parents to frequently run a practice in the backyard, in a park, at the beach, or at any available safe place.

- Parents often expect too much improvement from a child during a short tee ball season. If children say that they want to play again next year, the parents can anticipate seeing substantial progress based on the initial learning and playing experience and from the children's normal physical and social development. Off-season is a good time to have the kids practice basic skills, outside or indoors.

- Parents have to understand what their kids want from tee ball. Is it being with their friends? Getting a uniform? Learning how to play a real sport? Something more? Something less?

- Parents need to remember that sports are very different now from when they were kids. There is much more community organization for youth sports. A "sports parent" has become a job classification. Television and films have put a premium on competition and achieving. Tee ball provides a toned-down introduction to participation in a team game. Parents should welcome this opportunity and not try to accelerate their kids into a "winning is everything" state of mind. Enjoy these moments; they pass too quickly.

- Parental pressure for children to perform beyond their ability is bad for the players, the team, and the coach. Encouragement and a continuing focus on the fun of playing the game are more effective motivators.

T•BALL USA national survey

Advice for New Coaches

I believe the organization and coach play a vital role in setting the level of expectations. Especially with tee ball, *fun* and participation and player development are the top goals.

Parents should be cautious in expecting too much from their young athletes in the beginning and pressuring them to be successful too soon. It is important to experience the game and for the parent to provide positive guidance toward developing basic skills.

Reed Davis, Youth Sports Director, South Suburban Parks and Recreation, Fullerton, Colorado

school. Your responsibility in terms of the parents is to keep winning in perspective—it's only one part of the total experience. The parents' passion for victory should be tempered and not allowed to be the reason their kid plays tee ball.

Gender Issues

Tee ball participation in the United States is about 65 percent boys and 35 percent girls. Most leagues have mixed teams, although there are all-boys teams. There are also some all-girls teams that focus on preparing their players to move into girls' softball.

In terms of ability, there's little difference between boys and girls in the 4- and 5-year-old groups. Where variation exists, it's usually because some players have practiced more and thus perform better. At ages 6 and 7, the boys tend to be more competitive. There is no marked contrast in teamwork, especially when boys and girls are playing together. Coaches do report that concentration is significantly higher with girls of all ages, but there's a continual need for all the players to pay close attention to the action on the field. Boys do seem to respond better to criticism. Young girls are often more emotional and appear to accept comments better from female coaches (but not always). Criticism during practice or in a game from a player's own parent-coach sometimes creates immediate embarrassment or a problem at home for boys or girls. Negative comments should be handled at an appropriate time and place for all players and are not a gender matter.

Safety and Health

Sports medicine specialists have noted that participation in tee ball gives children the opportunity to learn teamwork while improving physical fitness and developing coordination. Tee ball, like other recreational activities, does expose children to some risk of injury. The use of safety helmets, softer balls, and the on-field presence of coaches and parents have kept the injury risk factor at a fraction of that in unorganized or informal play activities.

Dr. Letha Y. Griffin, of the Peachtree Orthopedic Clinic in Atlanta,

Boys and girls play very well together in tee ball. Many families have more than one child in a league program.

Georgia, is an authority on safety for youngsters entering sports. She has provided the following guidelines for decreasing the risk of player injury in tee ball.

Coaches of young children just beginning their sports career are in a very influential position. Their attitude toward sports will help shape the perceptions of the youngsters they instruct. As a coach, you can make the sport fun and safe.

- Have a group meeting with your players and their parents at the beginning of the season to discuss use of the equipment (especially bats, safety helmets, and the batting tee), the importance of following the rules, and the advantages of proper exercise, adequate rest, and good nutrition.
- Ask parents to see that the children get to bed on time on nights before practices and games. Tired kids, like tired adults, are not as alert as they need to be and will be more injury prone.
- Police the field before practices and games or establish a parent squad to do this. Pick up any broken glass or twigs or other potential hazards.
- Insist that all children arrive on time at practices and games so that they are not rushed but have time to warm up and mentally focus on playing ball. Injuries frequently occur because children are late and in a hurry and, therefore, not careful.
- Direct that all players are dressed appropriately with jewelry off, with footwear tied tightly, and with their equipment and water bottle.
- Encourage frequent water breaks during practices and between innings of a game.
- Establish early in the youngsters' sports career the importance of listening to the coaches and following the rules of the game. Trying to trip or otherwise injure an opposing team member should never be tolerated.
- Be positive in your instruction to children, as confident players are less frequently injured than timid, hesitant players.
- Be familiar with stretching and conditioning exercises that are appropriate for the age group you're coaching and incorporate these into practice and pregame warm-up activities.
- Never permit children to play when they are injured or sick. Alert parents if you suspect that a child is hurt; for example, if you see a player limping while running bases, make certain that the parents know their child is having a problem.
- Remove an injured player from the game and have ice applied to the injured part until medical help is available, if needed (see RICE sidebar next page).
- Have a cell phone available or note the location of a phone near the playing field in case an emergency occurs and help must be summoned. Be certain you know if any team member has a medical problem that might result in a medical emergency during play and be prepared for such situations. As an example, if a child is asthmatic, is diabetic, or has severe allergic reactions to bee or wasp stings, ask the parents what to do if the child develops such a reaction. Better yet, encourage the youngsters' parents to always be at practices and games. Medical crises can be minimized if a treatment or response plan has been established ahead of time.

Remember, you're a key figure. The attitude of the players and their parents will be shaped to a very large extent by what you say and do. Be a positive influence. Help ensure safety for kids entering sports and playing tee ball.

Questions and Answers

Q. Parents keep asking me if there's one thing they should tell their kids to help them be better tee ball players. Do you have any recommendations?

A. Here are two: Practice, and have fun; the best thing is to do both!

Q. How should I handle a parent who is unruly and creates a disturbance during a game?

A. Respond quickly. At a break in the action, speak to the parent and say that improper behavior sends a very negative message and will not be tolerated. If the parent has any issues to discuss, you can talk together after the game.

Q. How can I deal with a group of disruptive parents?

A. It's difficult to resolve this situation during a game when the coach is also a parent of a child on the team. This problem is best handled off the field by an appropriate individual from your league or the group that runs the tee ball program. A parents' meeting should be called to review the situation. An experienced coach from another team can also deal with the group. No players should be present. Both parents of each player need to be involved, for either parent can become unruly when seeing his or her child (often for the first time) involved in a

---

Minor Injuries? Think RICE

For minor sprains and strains, the RICE method will help a minor soft tissue injury heal faster.

- **Relative Rest.** Avoid activities that exacerbate the injury, but continue to move the injured area gently. Early gentle movement promotes healing.

- **Ice.** Apply ice to the affected area for 20 minutes; then leave it off for at least an hour. Do not use ice if the injured player has circulatory problems.

- **Compression.** Compression creates a pressure gradient that reduces swelling and promotes healing. An elastic bandage provides a moderate amount of pressure that will help discourage swelling.

- **Elevation.** Elevation is especially effective when used in conjunction with compression. Elevation provides a pressure gradient: the higher the injured body part is raised, the more fluid is pulled away from the injury site via gravity. Elevate the injury as high above the heart as comfortable. Continue to elevate intermittently until swelling is gone.

questionable or unpopular decision. Try to learn exactly what provoked the parents' anger. Is it a perception of bad umpiring? Is it something you did or didn't do? Does the team appear distracted or uninterested? Is there a valid reason for the parents' displeasure? Whatever the cause, the parents must be reminded of the influence their behavior has on their own child, the entire team, and the community. Settle the matter before the next game.

Q.   Can a family's request that their child play on my team with friends, neighbors, or siblings be accommodated?

A.   Check with your league. The answer usually is yes, as long as the skill level of all teams remain equal. This can be determined after tryouts or the first practice.

Q.   Is there one drill that's proven effective in minimizing any possible friction between a parent and child?

A.   There's a procedure that can be adapted to many drills. Divide the team into smaller groups (for example, if there are fifteen players, split them into three groups of five players). Assign two different parents to each group with the stipulation that their own child or children can't be in their group. During the practice of many defensive drills, the assigned parents stay with their group to help coach and assist the players.

PART TWO

Drills: The Foundation for Development, Success, Happiness, and a Coach's Peace of Mind

CHAPTER 9

Warm-Up Drills: Throwing, Fielding, and Baserunning

Here are some effective drills and skill-enhancement games from successful tee ball programs around the country. They are designed to warm up players' muscles in advance of more demanding exercise and also to generate enthusiasm. These drills cover the defensive skills of throwing, catching, fielding ground and fly balls, and running. Given the ages and attention spans of the participants, it is important that these activities also have fun content.

Throwing Drills

Show Me   W1

Purpose: To practice holding the ball and starting the throwing motion.

Have players show you that they are holding the ball with the thumb under the ball and with two or three fingers on top. Then each player quickly takes the throwing position with legs apart, the foot on the throwing-arm side behind the body, the throwing arm back and up, and the front shoulder turned toward the target. Repeat three times.

Use the L   W2

Purpose: To stress proper throwing-arm position.

Remind the players to have their throwing arm bent into the L shape. Separate the team into small groups and have the players throw to you and your assistants or volunteers, loudly calling out "L!" just before they throw the ball. If their catching skills are adequate, have players pair up with a partner standing about 10 feet away and throw to each other.

One-Knee Throws   W3

Purpose: To focus on one part of the throwing motion.

Players set one knee (on the same side as the throwing arm) on the ground. Their arm is brought up into the L position. The ball is held above

Throwing Tip from Coach Tom McClure

Players should always keep the elbow of their throwing arm as high as their shoulder when they throw. Make sure there is a 90-degree angle between the bicep and the forearm, or tell players to make an L as they throw, keeping their elbow up. Sometimes we call out, "Keep your elbow up!" or "Keep your hand away from your head!" or both. Never make a V, always an L.

Tom McClure, Northside Youth Organization, Atlanta, Georgia

and in front of the head, aimed toward the target. The nonthrowing hand rests on the other knee. Players reach back and throw to a partner or a coach. The wrist may bend slightly as the arm comes down; the body turns sideways. Use a soft tee ball or tennis ball. Begin this drill with a 12- to 15-foot distance. Increase it up to 20 feet as throwing skills improve. The ball can bounce en route to the target.

Bounce to the Bucket   W4

Purpose: To develop accuracy when throwing.

Place a large basket, open box, or plastic cooler on a base. Players try to throw or bounce a ball into the container. This can be done as a game, with players receiving 10 points for getting the ball in, 5 points for hitting the bucket, and 1 point for the nearest bounce, no matter where the ball finally stops. A favorite with kids, this drill primarily teaches throwing from the outfield to a base.

The **crow-hop** is a step and a little jump that provides momentum to throw.

Back Away   W5

Purpose: To develop arm strength.

Each player throws the ball to a partner and takes one step back after every throw. Start the drill with players 10 feet apart and continue moving away from each other until the ball cannot be caught before bouncing on the ground. If the drill is set up as a game, the pair that moves the greatest distance apart is the winner.

Crow-Hop   W6

Purpose: To practice a technique for generating momentum and increasing throwing power.

This is a classic drill practiced at all levels of baseball and softball. After fielding a ball, the player takes a short step forward on the foot opposite the throwing arm and hops in the direction of the intended target. The rear leg crosses over in front of the other and lands perpendicular to the target. Practice this procedure yourself before demonstrating it. Kids usually grasp the technique quickly and enjoy throwing from this forward motion.

Catching Drills

Catch   W7

Purpose: To master a basic defensive element.

Two or more players play catch. Start beginners with a rubber or sponge ball to reduce any fears of being hit by a ball. As soon as possible, progress to tennis balls, then to soft practice tee balls. To sustain interest, have the kids count the number of successful catches.

Catching Contest   W8

Purpose: To add some excitement while improving catching skills.

Players are in pairs and stand about 10 feet apart. When a coach calls out "Throw!," one partner throws the ball overhand to the other. The pair that can throw the ball back and forth the most times without dropping it wins. In close contests, the distance can be increased as the match progresses.

Catching Flies   W9

Purpose: To develop the skill of catching balls hit in the air and to minimize player apprehension.

Hit or throw fly balls to fielders at all positions by using a rubber ball, tennis ball, or soft tee ball. Repetition and practice are the keys to progress and success.

Throwing and Catching Drills

In the game of One and Two, this catch will score no points, but the player's "pinkies down" form is excellent.

One and Two   W10

Purpose: To practice accurate throwing and capable catching.

Two teammates play catch. The thrower scores 2 points if the ball is caught at or above the shoulders and 1 point if the ball is caught between the shoulders and the waist. There are no points scored if the ball is caught below the receiver's waist. The first player to score 10 points wins.

Back and Forth   W11

Purpose: To practice throwing and catching a ball.

Split the team into two groups. The players stand side by side in two facing lines. Adjust the distance between the lines according to the experience and skills of the players. The first player in one line throws to the first player in the other line. After the ball is tossed, the thrower runs to the end of the line, and the other players all move up one place. The receiver catches the ball, throws it to the new first player in line in the other group, and goes to the end of the line. If (when) the ball is not caught, restart the drill with the intended receiver. The drill is over when every player has thrown and caught a ball.

Relay W12

Purpose: To learn how to move the ball from the outfield to the bases or home plate.

Split the team into groups of three or four players who stand about 10 feet apart in a single line. The player at the head of the line throws a ball to the second in line. After catching the ball, the second player turns and throws to the third in line. The drill continues to the end of the line; then the throws are relayed back, player by player, to the original end. The drill proceeds until the ball makes a complete trip in one direction without a bad throw or a dropped catch. If (when) the ball is not caught, restart the drill by returning the ball to the player who was attempting to complete the relay.

Diamond Drill W13

Purpose: To develop teamwork and practice throwing and catching.

Divide the team into four groups (call them A, B, C, and D or four different colors). Station one player from each group at the pitching area and at first, second, and third base. Player A (in the pitching area) throws a tee ball to player A at first base, who throws it to player A at second base, who throws the ball to player A at third base, who returns the ball back to player A in the pitching area. Players call out their letter or color as they throw and catch the ball. Players in the other groups spread out to allow room for throwing and catching, and they retrieve any wayward balls for group A. The procedure is repeated with the B, C, and D groups. Repeat the same sequence three times.

Variation: Eliminate the players at third base (so each group has three players). You can also reverse the direction in which the ball is thrown.

Moving Target W14

Purpose: To practice catching skills at a higher level.

This drill is done in pairs. Before each throw, the receiver varies the location of the target by moving from side to side or forward or backward. Standing, one-knee (short- and long-range) W3 , and crow-hop W6 overhand throws should be included in the drill.

Fielding Drills

Crab Drill W15

Purpose: To improve response to oncoming ground balls.

Each player stands in the basic fielding stance, crouched forward with glove open and down. A coach rolls or hits a ball to various infield locations. The player closest to the moving ball takes three or four steps, traps the ball, and returns it to the coach. Rotate player positions during the drill.

Scoop or Pickup W16

Purpose: To practice essential fielding action.

Two players (or two rows of players) line up about 10 feet apart. From a kneeling position, one player rolls or bounces the ball for the opposite player to trap. Repeat ten times in each direction.

Mini-Pepper W17

Purpose: To practice fielding the ball.

This is a modification of a classic baseball-softball drill. A coach hits a ball to one of three fielders positioned by the coach. Repeat ten times. Rotate player positions.

Left: Crab drill action.

Right: "Hey, Coach, hit me a ball!"

Distraction   W18

Purpose: To improve concentration.

A coach rolls a ball to a fielder, but another player runs in front of the fielder and tries to break that player's concentration on getting the ball. Instruct the runner to avoid a collision.

Dive   W19

Purpose: To practice determined fielding.

A coach hits or throws a ball to one side of a fielder, who has to lunge to get the ball. After the ball is secured, the player throws it to a base.

Just Block It   W20

Purpose: To improve fielding skills.

A coach hits a ball directly to an infielder, who tries to prevent the ball from getting through to the outfield. The play is successful if the ball is stopped (it's even better if it's caught).

Variation: Turn it into a game, with 1 point scored for every block, 2 points for a catch, and no points if the ball is not stopped. Individual players or the entire team can earn points, and the totals can be compared during the season.

Sometimes only a bare hand is needed to field a ball.

Bare Hand   W21

Purpose: To practice an alternate fielding technique.

A hit tee ball often stops moving along the ground before a player gets to it. Set a ball about 5 feet in front of a fielder. The player runs up to the motionless ball, picks it up with the bare hand, and throws it to first or second base. Rotate the drill among all the defensive players.

The Triangle   W22

Purpose: To practice good footwork and movement to either side when fielding.

Three players (or a coach and two players) form a triangle. The space between the participants can be between 10 and 20 feet, depending on the experience of the teammates. A player or coach at one point of the triangle rolls or bounces a ball from a kneeling-down position to the left or right of one of the other players. The receiver fields the ball and throws it to the third player, who relays it back to the point where the drill originated. If three players are involved without a coach, rotate the starting point of the drill. The thrower does not identify the receiver before the play.

Reverse W23
Purpose: To teach fielders how to safely catch a fly ball hit behind them.

Players line up facing the coach from 5 to 10 feet away. They first learn a pattern of steps: they take one step back, one to the side, and then they turn around and run back (never backward) to catch the ball. Players are told to look up or back for a moment by turning their head to watch the path of the ball in flight. Then the coach calls out a player's name, points in the general direction of where the ball will be thrown, and tosses the ball up, over, and behind the player. As the players' fielding skills develop, eliminate the pointing. The team can be split into smaller groups to allow more fielding opportunities for each player.

The Wall W24
Purpose: To practice fielding the ball.

One player throws a rubber or cloth ball against a wall and then catches it on the fly or after one bounce.

Variation: Have another player or adult throw the ball. This drill can be performed at home or at any wall in a safe area.

Catchers' Drills

Go Get W25
Purpose: To develop the catcher's fielding skills.

Have younger or beginning players in the position of catcher practice running after a ball that has been hit to the part of the infield just past the playing line. A coach rolls a ball to the left or right of the pitching area. The catcher runs out, secures the ball, and throws it to first base. To best simulate a game situation, other players are positioned in the pitching area and at third base so the catcher learns to avoid collisions with infielders. In this situation, the first player to reach the ball calls "I've got it!"

Protect the Plate W26
Purpose: To prevent an offensive player from crossing home plate.

Only an older or more experienced player should be allowed to try to tag a base runner coming in to home plate from third base. In this drill the catcher receives the ball from an infielder, stands to one side of the base path, and tries to tag a player who is running to home plate. Don't allow the catcher to stand directly in the runner's way, and explain the danger of obstructing the runner.

Note: In many tee ball programs, the coach of the defensive team steps in, receives the ball, and tries to make the play in a safe manner. The runner often evades the tag.

Baserunning Drills

Remind the players to run on the balls of their feet and to swing their arms.

Who's on First?   W27
Purpose: To focus attention on each player's running skills.

One player stands at home plate. When a coach calls "Start!," the player runs to first base at top speed. Watch to see that the player is running with correct form (see pages 45–46). The drill can also be done between two bases or from third base to home plate.

What Now?   W28
Purpose: To learn baserunning strategy.

Without holding a bat, a player swings and then runs from home plate to first base. The coach stationed there calls out instructions as the runner approaches the base (such as "Stay here!" or "Run to second base!"). Repetition with varying commands will reinforce the players' knowledge of what to do when they safely get to first base.

Run Down   W29
Purpose: To simulate a game baserunning situation.

Two fielders try to tag out a runner, who is attempting to advance from one base to another without being tagged. The fielders throw a ball back and forth and chase after the runner, trying to touch the runner with the ball. Players rotate positions and repeat the drill.

Track Meet   W30
Purpose: To practice running speed and form.

Position two players at home plate. When a coach yells "Start!," one player runs to first base, the other to third base. They continue running (in opposite directions) around the bases. The first runner to return to home plate is the winner.

Note: To avoid collisions, tell the runner who goes to first base to step on second base from the outside corner. The other runner, coming from third base, is to step on the inside corner of second base. Have an assistant coach or volunteer at second base to direct traffic.

Catch the Coach   W31
Purpose: To improve conditioning and player-coach interaction.

A coach or assistant coach runs from home plate to first base. After a head start of a few steps, the coach shouts "Tag me!" to a player holding a ball, who then runs after the coach and tries to touch him or her with the ball. The coach decides where, when, or if the runner is successful.

Catch the Players   W32

Purpose: To improve conditioning and team-coach interaction.

A coach starts out four or more players at 10-second intervals. Players run from home plate and start to circle the bases. The coach starts last and tries to tag the runners or snatch off their caps.

Note: Run this drill with only one group at each practice to avoid taking too much time (and coach fatigue).

Catch the Team   W33

Purpose: To improve conditioning and player-coach bonding.

This drill is the same as Catch the Players (W32), except the coach runs after the entire team. The team starts running as one group, and is given a 10-second head start by the coach. This is a team favorite and is usually eagerly anticipated as the practice-ending event.

CHAPTER 10

Defensive Drills: Infield Play, Outfield Play, and Team Defense

Success in tee ball may best be measured by the quality of a team's defense. Often, as many batters reach first base due to poor fielding as they do from solid hits. And many runners only advance safely because of sloppy or careless defense. Hitting is a role played by one player at a time; defense is an expression of teamwork. This chapter offers proven drills that will help your players develop their defensive skills. Also, always remind players to "think ahead" about what to do if a ball comes their way.

Infield Drills

First Base–Third Base D1

Purpose: To practice fielding ground and thrown balls.

Divide the team into two groups, one lined up behind and about 10 feet to the right of first base facing home plate, and the other lined up behind and about 10 feet to the left of third base. Station a coach or assistant about 15 feet in front of each base. Increase the distance as the players' fielding skills improve. To begin, the coach near first base throws a ground ball toward the first player in line behind the base. The player fields the ball and then runs with the ball to step on the base, simulating a tag out.

In the second part of the drill, the same fielder is set in fielding position near the bag and runs to it, ready to catch a ball thrown by the coach. (Note: Throwing the ball as opposed to hitting it with a bat is preferred as it will be more accurate and travel at less speed.) Run these two stages of the drill with each player in line at first base.

Simultaneously, the coach at third base conducts the same procedure. When all the players have had an opportunity to field both parts of the drill, the two groups and their coaches switch places. While the coaches are working with the players at first and third bases, another coach or volunteer can be working with the shortstop and second-base player; see D2 .

Shortstop–Second Base D2

Purpose: To practice fielding ground and thrown balls.

As players complete **D1** , they move to second base, where one player becomes a shortstop and one a second-base player. The coach near second base throws the ball on the ground toward the second-base player. That player fields the ball while the shortstop runs over to second base, stepping with one foot on the corner of the base that faces the outfield. The second-base player throws the fielded ball to the shortstop now standing on the base.

In the second part, the drill reverses. The coach rolls the ball to the shortstop, who fields it and throws to the second-base player covering the bag. Do this drill twice with each fielder.

Fastest Fingers D3

Purpose: To improve reflex action, ballhandling, throwing, and quickness.

Line up five fielders side by side behind the playing line and facing home plate. Have an assistant place a tee ball 10 feet in front of each player. The coach at home plate calls "Go!" and then starts counting out loud, "1001, 1002, 1003 . . . " The first player charges the ball, picks it up with the bare hand, and throws it to the coach. The count stops when the fielder has thrown the ball. The routine is repeated for the other four players. Another group of five replaces them until the entire team has participated in the drill. The fielder with the fastest time (lowest number) to complete the drill wins the Fastest Fingers title.

This player demonstrates an athletic bare-handed pickup in the Fastest Fingers drill.

Outfield Drills

I've Got It D4

Purpose: To practice teamwork (and safety) when catching fly balls.

Split the team into two groups and have them form two lines about 25 feet apart in the outfield. A coach hits or throws a ball in the air between the first players in each line. While the ball is in flight, the outfielder closest to where the ball appears to be coming down calls, "I've got it!" The other fielder moves to a backup position. Repeat the drill until one player in each line has called for and caught a fly ball.

To Second Base D5

Purpose: To work on getting the ball from the outfield to the infield.

Position two of your more experienced or older players at second base and shortstop. Divide the remainder of the team into three groups and assign one coach or assistant to each group. The players in each group stand in line in the outfield at left, center, and right field. Starting in right field, the first outfielder in line throws a ball to second base. The shortstop moves over to second base to catch the ball. The second-base player stands on the first-base side of second base, facing the outfield and prepared to retrieve errant throws. Each outfielder in the line throws a ball to second base. Repeat this drill with the group in center field. Repeat the drill with the left field group, but this time the second-base player runs to cover the base, and the shortstop faces left field.

Team Defense

Dee-Fense D6

Purpose: To practice putting base runners out.

Place eight players on the field at first, second, and third base, shortstop, pitcher, and the three outfield positions. The rest of the team (preferably the younger or beginning players) serve as base runners.

A coach about to hit a fungo in defensive team practice.

The action always begins with base runners on first and second base. The coach at home plate throws the ball randomly to each fielder as the runners try to advance. The fielders catch the ball and try to get the runners out. The home plate coach acts as catcher. Before the ball is thrown, the defense should shout the next situation, such as "The play's at second base!" Make certain that each player handles the ball at least twice. If time permits, rotate the base runners with the defense.

Fun-Go D7

Purpose: To practice fielding in a simulated game situation.

A *fungo* is a ball batted by a coach in practice situations. A tee is not used; the batter tosses the ball up in the air before hitting it. For this drill, place players at first, second, and third base, shortstop, pitcher, and the three outfield positions. There are no other defensive players on the field. Any additional teammates will be used as base runners and rotated into the defense during the drill. If only nine or fewer players are available, use assistants or volunteers as base runners.

A coach begins the action by hitting a fungo. Be prepared with examples of various possible offensive actions and the proper defensive moves for each. Try to hit a ball to every player at least one time.

Variation: The drill can also be performed as "Ghost Fun-Go." In this version, there are no base runners. All of the defensive players are on the field, and the coach tells them to imagine where he has placed invisible offensive players and where to throw the ball.

Pizza Slices   D8

Purpose: To teach fielders to stay and play in their positions.

Mark out three lines on the field from home plate: one extending into the outfield halfway between first and second base, one through second base and into the outfield, and one into the outfield halfway between second and third base. This creates four zones, one for each base player, the shortstop, and outfielders. Instruct them all to stay in their assigned areas. If you have extra infielders, they should back up the four primary players. The pitcher fields any fair balls past the playing line if they can be reached before another position player gets them. Outfielders also remain within their "slice" of the playing field. The center fielder may cover either of the two middle zones but only the areas closest to the middle of the playing field. Drill your

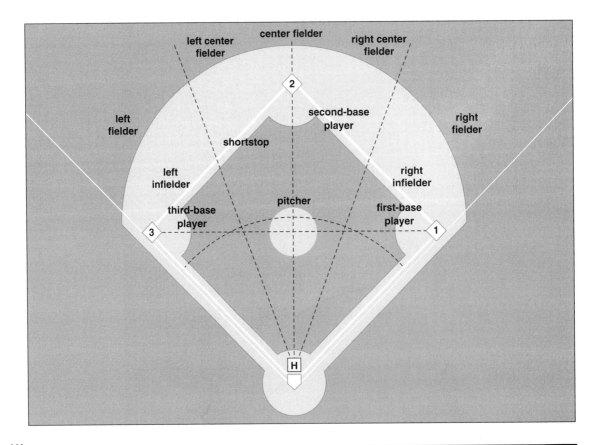

Alligator Drill

I am a tee ball coach and want to tell you about a drill that worked for my team for catching ground balls. Since kids have a tendency to use only their gloves, I practiced my team with "alligators." I demonstrated with a glove on one hand held down near the ground and my throwing hand held closely above it. The glove and open hand simulate an alligator's mouth. The players charge and "chomp" the oncoming ball just as an alligator gobbles up a meal. This way, the fielders get in front of the ball and use their bare hand to keep the ball in the glove.

Tee ball kids are, to me, the most rewarding age group to teach. They can learn so much if you know how to keep their attention! Drills such as Alligator really help. What you teach your players is the foundation on which they will build and perfect their skills. Also, their future coaches will appreciate the good habits you can instill in the children from the beginning.

Cheryl K. Shahan, Woodlawn Little League, Woodlawn, Tennessee

team by hitting or rolling a ball into the different zones until the players learn to stay in their designated positions. Keep reminding them not to leave their zones. Don't expect perfection; the excitement of a game often replaces actions learned in practice.

Questions and Answers

Q. I have a situation where another coach has taught his pitchers to field the ball and run toward the batter with the ball in hand to tag the hitter out. In three of four instances, the tag to the runner heading to first base was on the left shoulder. The pitcher's momentum did push one runner down. The impact did not cause serious injury except for skin abrasions, but the runner's parents were understandably upset. When I approached that coach, he said he "saw nothing wrong" with the defensive play, and "it's just baseball." I can accept this action in an older age group, but we have 7-year-olds knocking down 5-year-olds. Is there a rule concerning tagging the player with the ball?

A. The other coach should instruct his pitcher to secure the ball and throw it to first base to try to get the batter out. That's why the first-base player is positioned there. If the ball hasn't passed the playing line, it's not a fair ball, and there's no play. If the ball is in play, it will be very difficult for the pitcher to field the ball and run to tag the hitter en route to first base (unless the hitter is v-e-r-y s-l-o-w). A runner is out if tagged by a fielder while running to a base when the ball is in play. Base runners are not out if they have to run outside the base path to avoid interfering with a fielding attempt. Defensive players who field a ball should try to throw the ball to a base to which a player is running. If the fielder is close to the oncoming or passing runner, sure, tag for the out. Otherwise, use teamwork: field the ball and throw to a base. A fielder chasing a runner in an attempt to tag happens all the time. Instruct your kids to involve the other defensive players.

In the absence of a rule prohibiting the action you describe, encourage the other coach to have his pitcher field the ball and throw to first base. The pitcher can also retrieve the ball and try to step on first base before the batter arrives, but there's still some possibility of body contact in that action.

Q. Drills are not as exciting or as much fun as games. How can I keep the players interested?

A. To help, rotate the players' positions, which creates change (different location, different players to stand next to, different fielding responsibility, etc.). This usually brings them back into a more responsive manner. If necessary, speak to the parents. Enthusiasm and cheers of support can have an immediate effect in practice sessions and in games.

CHAPTER 11

Batting Drills

The four basic elements of hitting—grip, stance, swing, and follow-through—are covered in chapter 4, pages 38–40. This section includes advice and drills on batting from several of the most successful tee ball coaches in the country.

Try not to give the players too many instructions at one time because this can create confusion. As an example, some batters become more concerned with their stance than with actually hitting the ball. At the first practice, let every player try just three times to hit the ball off the tee. Take notes. At the next practice, show the team—collectively and individually—the batting fundamentals. Expect style and performance variations, for your team will have a range of differences in age, height, weight, strength, concentration, skill, confidence, expectations, attitude, and other physical and personality traits. Don't attempt to mold a group of players to all hit the same way. Instill good hitting habits; spot the bad ones and correct them. Most kids have a natural swing, so if they are hitting the ball well, don't overcoach.

Older players have a tendency to want to launch a ball up off the tee. They enjoy getting the ball to arc high in the air and think it's a really good hit. In the more advanced or experienced leagues, the fly ball is often caught for an out. To compensate, instruct these capable batters to try to hit line drives every other time they are at bat.

Invisible Bat B1

Purpose: To teach the essential movements of the batting sequence.

The players are widely spaced in a row pretending to hold a bat while facing an imaginary tee. At the call of "Swing!" players simulate the batting sequence, from taking the stance to the follow-through and dropping the bat. Repeat ten times, maximum. This drill is excellent as an at-home exercise, outdoors or inside.

Invisible Ball B2

Purpose: To simulate hitting off the tee.

This drill is similar to B1 , but each player swings a real bat toward an actual tee. The ball is the imaginary element. The batter tries to move the bat through the space where the ball would be if it were on the tee. Sometimes the swing will be too high; often the tee will be knocked over. It's more important for the coach to evaluate the full batting motion than to be concerned that the invisible ball was or wasn't hit.

Tee Time B3

Purpose: To practice hitting off the tee.

This is the most important batting drill. The coach works with each batter—adjusts the tee, places a ball on the tee, steps away, and calls "Hit!" Your comments on the effort and suggestions for improvement should be made after every swing. Repeat the drill five times.

Variation: Have the batter run to first base after the final hit.

Tee Time. Coach and batter work together to develop hitting skills.

Numbers B4

Purpose: To practice hitting off the tee.

Separate the team into three groups, each with a batting tee and an assistant or qualified volunteer. The groups work simultaneously and need to be spaced well apart in the field. Each player bats for three or four minutes while the other players in the group field the balls. (This provides batting and fielding practice at the same time.) After all the players have batted, each tee is assigned a number: 1, 2, or 3. Have the assistant call out the numbers randomly. Only a batter at that tee can hit at that time. The players take turns, waiting to hear the number of their tee called. This part of the drill allows the coach to watch each player individually.

Coach Says B5

Purpose: To practice the basic parts of the batting routine.

This drill is a variation of B1 and is similar to the game of Simon Says. The coach rapidly calls out one of five commands in random sequence. Any players who do not correctly perform the action requested or do another motion (or nothing at all) have to sit down. The drill continues until only one player is standing. The coach alternates between the following calls:

- **Hands:** players grip the imaginary bat with their knuckles up
- **Feet:** players jump with their feet apart facing a make-believe tee
- **Stance:** players assume the batting position with arms raised up toward the rear shoulder
- **Squash the bug:** players step, swing, and rotate on the ball of their back foot (heel up) as if stepping on a bug
- **Swing:** players perform complete batting action, including dropping the imaginary bat

Details to Monitor

There are two elements for effective hitting to observe with every player during batting practice.

In the stance position:

- The ball should be opposite the belly button for most players. (Some batters hit better off a higher tee setting.)
- The feet should be spread apart directly below the shoulders.
- The front foot is set even with the tee or further back.
- The bat is pointed up and tilted backward.

During the swing:

- The front foot steps toward the pitching area.
- The arms move from shoulder to shoulder and are kept straight at the point of contact with the ball.

This player shows good swing and follow-through form. Note the level bat and proper foot placement.

- The back foot rotates with the heel off the ground.
- The batter's eyes must stay focused on the ball; the head remains stationary.

At-Home Drills

Skills practiced away from the field, away from the coach and the assistants, away from teammates, and in a familiar and noncompetitive setting can be a positive and fun experience.

Individual practice sessions can provide special benefits because they bring the parents (or other family members or adults) directly into the tee ball activity. But it's crucial that the adults understand both what to instruct and how to approach the opportunity to participate in the young player's development.

Remind the adults to be positive, remain patient, and have realistic expectations. The drills and related activities can be held at home (some of them indoors) or in a nearby open area, park, or schoolyard. Games between adult and child are especially effective. Suggest that the parents offer a small treat or reward after practice (ice cream, chore elimination, etc.).

Some of the off-the-field drills for skill improvement are similar to those described elsewhere in this book but are modified for use by adults who aren't coaches for individual player practice. Adults should do the drills with the players, if possible. If siblings or neighbor kids are available, have them participate as well. The workout should not exceed 30 minutes for younger players, unless the child is having fun and wants to continue. At-home drills for older players can be one hour. In either case, tell the child about how long the practice will be. Relate the time to the length of a favorite TV program. Not every drill needs to be practiced at each session.

Adults should keep a record of the day's activity and report back to the coach which drills have the most or least effect on the child's skill development.

Warm-Up Exercises

It's important that all participants warm up their muscles before attempting more complex movements. Start with the following warm-ups.

- **Stretching:** Shake arms and legs. Swing arms and twist back and forth. Bend and touch toes.

- **Running:** Run around the house or yard or to a tree or some point-to-point distance.

- **Jumping jacks:** Clap hands overhead while jumping up with legs apart. Move the hands to the sides while jumping again and closing the legs.

Throwing Drills

Start by reminding the child how to hold the ball (see The Grip, page 43) before releasing it. Carefully, go through the basic throwing movements (see The Motion, pages 43–44), covering where the legs are to be, where to look, what the throwing arm does, and how to release the ball. Have the child throw five times.

- **Show Me.** The child demonstrates the proper grip and uses the L position to throw correctly five times. The parent returns the throw by also making the L and calling attention to proper arm action. **W1**

- **Bounce to the Bucket.** Do this activity as a game, parent versus child. **W4**

- **Back Away.** The parent and child throw to one another, both counting the catches out loud. **W5**

Catching Drills

The parent throws the ball to the child, mixing up the route of the ball. (See Ground Balls and Fly Balls, pages 41–42). Practice each drill a minimum of five times.

Tee ball mom and tee ball kid practice throwing and catching.

- **Catch.** Count the number of good catches. Repeat until at least five are successfully caught. **W7**

- **Moving Target.** The parent uses overhand or underhand delivery from a standing position. **W14**

Throwing and Catching Drills

- **One and Two.** This drill is only for the older and more experienced players. **W10**

- **The Wall.** This can be done anywhere there is a wall against which a parent can throw a ball. **W24**

Running Drills

The child starts by running in place. The parent checks that the player runs on the balls of the feet and with the arms swinging.

- **Catch the Player(s).** An adult (or older sibling or friend) gives the child a head start and tries to tag the child before the youngster reaches a prede termined spot (e.g.: tree, glove on ground). **W32**

- **Time Trial.** The child runs to or between two measured spots (around a house, to the corner and back, between two trees or thrown-down objects). Time is kept, and the child's progress is recorded after every at-home drill.

Batting Drills

The parent focuses on a repetition of the basic techniques for hitting the ball off the tee (see Batting, pages 38–40).

- **Batting tee:** The parent adjusts the tee to the height of the child.

- **Grip:** The child's hands are together, above the knob. Remind the child not to squeeze the bat.

- **Stance:** The child bends at the knees in a slight crouch, with weight on the balls of the feet.

- **Swing:** The child's swing should be level and hit through the ball, completing the swing.

- **Feet:** Check the positions of the child's feet before, during, and after the swing.

- **Eyes:** Remind the child to keep the eyes on the ball and keep the head down.

- **Follow-through:** The child should extend the arms, swing around, and drop the bat.

- **Invisible Bat** and **Invisible Ball.** The player can practice these drills alone, without adult supervision. **B1** **B2**

AT-HOME DRILLS

Pre-tee ball players and their younger siblings can practice hitting at home with innovative training devices that are designed to make early-age skill training both effective and fun.

Great for beginners, this plastic tee ball set includes an easy-to-use bat, oversize balls, and an adjustable-height batting tee that adapts to a child's developing skills.   Little Tikes

Safety

Hitting a ball on the playing field or at home should always be a matter of concern to parents. In tee ball, youngsters swing bats, chase balls, and run around having fun. The tee ball player's young siblings will be curious but need to be kept some distance away from at-home batting practice. Suggest to parents that they use older family members, neighborhood kids, or even the family dog to retrieve the balls. Tee balls can also be hit toward a wall or a fence. A practice tee with the ball attached by a nylon cord is available at many sporting goods stores.

This Is for All the Parents

At first I was a mom watching my children play tee ball, and then I became the assistant coach. Next I was the head coach. Now I have been our organization's tee ball director for seven years. The one thing I always tell the parents is to try to adapt at home what the kids are learning on the field. For example, I often found that the beginning children were somewhat afraid of the ball. Even if it is a safety ball with a sponge core, it looks like a hard ball, and many kids are scared to catch it. I have the parents take tennis rackets and hit some tennis balls to their children. They will go after the balls without any fear, and eventually the at-home drill can be switched over to using practice (slightly softer) tee balls. The parents can also tell their kids to pretend that there is a camera in their glove and to follow the ball until it is caught. Parents and coaches should remember one thing: the children are just that—children. Without direction, at home or on the field, they will usually do what they want to do and when they want to do it. Pack your patience. It can be a long season.

Robin Hosey, Tee Ball Director, Keansburg Baseball and Softball, Keansburg, New Jersey

Questions and Answers

Q. How do I help my son to stop swinging the bat down on the ball?

A. Try this: Raise the tee to neck height and slowly lower it after every level swing; put a black dot with a marker pen at the lower third of the ball, and tell him to aim at the dot. This should help him swing parallel to the ground, even up a bit. How about an incentive? Make a game of it: have your son swing ten times; if five are level, give him a treat.

Q. At the first parent meeting I was asked several times for a simple backyard drill to teach 4-year-olds how to catch a ball. Can you recommend one?

A. Use tennis or rubber balls; no glove is required. Stand about 5 feet from the child and throw underhand. Vary the arc of the toss. Tell the child to catch the ball with both hands. The key to catching is the elimination of fear from seeing an oncoming ball and concentration. A young player will eventually be able to catch once a few basic elements are coordinated.

APPENDIX: Activity Survey

T•BALL USA surveyed a representative sample of tee ball league organizers and administrators and coaches from parks and recreation departments, YMCAs, Boys & Girls Clubs, local units of national and regional youth baseball organizations, and independent, nonaligned (usually parent-run) groups. The responses summarized below will provide information for coaches and others concerned with building successful programs in their communities.

Things That Make Programs Work

- an emphasis on participation and fun
- fair and equal treatment of all players
- dependable volunteers and parental participation
- an atmosphere of enjoyment and learning
- coaches and parents with good attitudes
- quality supervisors
- an experienced team manager
- handling problems immediately
- good communication between coaches and parents
- support from local community
- equipment that lasts
- no individual statistics recorded
- certificates of participation for all players
- certificates of appreciation for coaches
- a short season (eight to ten games for youngest players)
- balanced teams
- a parent meeting before season starts
- letting parents stand on field with child during first few practices and first game
- good practice and playing field conditions
- rainy day indoor practice alternatives
- a priority on safety
- appropriate postgame snacks and beverages

Biggest Problems with Parents

- trying to push kids too hard and too fast; expectations too high
- scheduling conflicts
- not familiar with game rules and league regulations
- putting more pressure on kids and seeking more intense competition
- trying to relive their childhood through their kids
- not prepared to volunteer; inconsiderate of volunteers' time
- dropping off kids (sometimes late) and not staying to help

- overzealous rooting
- forgetting that the game is a learning process for children
- not appreciating coaches and league officials
- forgetting there are other kids on the team
- talking to the coaches during games
- not having time to play and practice with their kids at home
- overinvolved
- not involved enough

Biggest Problems with Kids

- short attention span; not staying focused
- parents and grandparents
- not motivated to practice and improve
- equipment wrong size
- too many converging on a hit ball
- teasing and taunting
- lack of respect for authority
- little baseball knowledge
- having too many other activities
- "video game" mind-set

How Families Learn about Program

- locating and calling league
- printed handout
- local media
- word of mouth
- notices displayed at supermarkets, schools, and community centers
- talking to currently or previously involved parents
- company and organization bulletin boards
- inquiring at local parks and recreation departments
- inquiring at sporting goods stores that equip teams

Biggest Needs

- soliciting sponsors
- fund-raising plans
- new equipment
- general game information
- dedicated practice and game site
- underwriting uniform costs
- professional safety tips from local source
- local publicity about the program
- news about other leagues
- printed material for coaches and parents

Popular Special Events

- end-of-season party
- participation awards ceremony
- parents versus kids game
- exhibition game at a community event

T•BALL USA Association

The T•BALL USA Association is the national nonprofit youth sports organization dedicated to the development of the game of tee ball as an introduction to baseball and softball. Its mission is to

- assist national, regional, and local youth baseball leagues and nonaligned community groups to maximize their existing tee ball activity or to introduce the sport in their area
- stimulate participation by young boys and girls in an early-age organized team game and instill a foundation for sportsmanship, fair play, and teamwork
- bring together community and parent groups, municipal departments or agencies, service organizations, and leagues now involved or interested in the sport so that the game may be played in an informed and consistent manner in all parts of the country
- provide printed and electronic communications and guidelines to those responsible for the local administration of the game, the coaches, and the participants' families
- recommend rules of play and related procedures
- establish equipment specifications
- create avenues of support with companies interested in advancing youth and family-oriented activities
- oversee T•BALL USA Academy functions, including camps and clinics
- publicize and promote the sport in all appropriate ways

Left: A tee ball team runs onto the field with the Oakland A's as part of a T•BALL USA event.
Oakland Athletics

Right: Thousands of tee ball kids and their families and coaches are invited to T•BALL USA activities at Major and Minor League ballparks. Oakland Athletics

The T•BALL USA logo is used to identify the projects, services, and events created to support national and local programs, mark official licensed products and corporate relationships, and serves as a connecting link for the tee ball constituency. See the resources section for contact information.

Coaching Checklist

For your convenience, here's a reminder of things to do.

Before Practices or Games

- inspect the field for any safety hazards
- locate first-aid kit
- check that batting tees are stable and in good working order
- be sure enough safety helmets are available
- observe team warm-up exercises

On the Practice Field: Defense

First base: show the first-base player where to stand when no runner is on base; have player practice by infielders throwing to first base

Second base: position player; have player practice fielding plays, such as tagging a runner out

Shortstop; right and **left infielders:** show proper positions; have players practice by fielding balls and throwing to first or second base for an out

Third base: show position; have player practice action, such as diving to knock down ball

Pitcher: player stands in pitcher's area but acts as infielder; have player practice action, such as fielding ball and throwing to catcher to force out runner coming from third base

Catcher: player stands behind and away from home plate until ball is hit (after ball is hit, adult removes tee and bat, and catcher moves up to cover plate); have player practice action, such as tagging base runner out and throwing to first base

General infield: remind infielders to stay behind playing line until ball is hit; have players attempt double plays, catch short fly balls, tag runners on the base paths, relay ball from an outfielder to a base and to the catcher; show players where to play and what to do if the ball comes toward them; encourage kids to give vocal support to teammates

Outfielders: position players; have players practice catching fly balls in a crowd (remind them to call "I've got it!"), catching ground balls and throwing to infield, having one outfielder get a relay from another outfielder and throw to an infielder; remind kids to give vocal support to teammates

On the Practice Field: Offense

Batter: give basic hitting instructions; have players practice hitting the ball and dropping bat properly, running to first base

Base runner: instruct action at first base (coach at first base should signal whether to run past first base or turn toward second base); remind players that a forced runner on base must advance and a nonforced runner can hold position on base; players on base must watch what the next batter does and where the ball goes; have players practice sliding

Off the Field

Preseason Meeting with Parents

- outline overall program
- review parents' responsibilities
- discuss expectations, value of patience
- cover the dos and don'ts at practices and games
- advise them about questions their kids may ask them
- tell them not to blame the officials
- outline league-specific information
- distribute printed materials

Preseason Meeting with Team

Also review the following at the first practice and as needed.

- review the playing field and the positions
- demonstrate the batting tee
- explain the basic rules
- briefly outline what will happen at practices and games
- explain important safety matters
- emphasize that tee ball is a fun and active game
- add other comments as needed

Pregame Meeting with Team

- provide motivation
- remind players that they must play fair, follow the rules, listen for instructions, call for the ball, and must not throw the bat or all run to field the same ball
- remind players it's only a game, and they should have fun: tee ball is a game for kids
- add other comments as needed

Postpractice and Postgame Meeting with Team

- listen to their chatter
- summarize the day's activity
- be specific; no generalities

- recognize and praise progress and individual success
- note any humorous things that happened
- answer questions
- tell them when and where the next practice or game will be
- explain a drill(s) for them to do at home
- add other comments as needed

Postpractice and Postgame Meeting with Parents

- listen to their comments and questions
- resolve problems as quickly as possible
- if needed, ask for help with specific matters
- explain drill(s) you've given the kids to practice at home
- tell them when and where the next practice or game will be

Remember, you're the coach. Go home and reflect on the positive elements. Think about what could be improved upon and begin to plan for the next practice or game.

Glossary

At bat: A player is "at bat" when it is his turn to try to hit the ball.

Bag: See *base*.

Ball: In coach-pitch, a ball thrown out of the batter's range that the batter doesn't attempt to hit. (*Note:* There are no walks in tee ball.)

Base: A square white slab set at three corners of the infield to mark first, second, and third base. See also *home plate*.

Base coach: A coach, parent, or other adult volunteer positioned in foul territory near first or third base.

Base hit: Any hit ball tht results in the batter safely reaching base without an *error* or a *fielder's choice* being made on the play.

Base on balls: An award of first base granted to the batter who, during the time *at bat*, receives four errant pitches. Also called a "walk." (*Note:* This does not apply to tee ball.)

Base path: The running lane for base runners.

Base runner: A batter becomes a base runner when the ball is put into play.

Bases loaded: The game status when a runner is on each of the bases.

Bat-around: A playing procedure of the game where the entire offensive team bats during an inning.

Batter: The offensive player at bat.

Batter's box: A rectangle, marked in chalk, on both sides of home plate that defines where the batter stands.

Batting helmet: See *safety helmet*.

Batting order: The order, determined by the coach, in which players take their turns at bat.

Batting tee: A freestanding flexible and adjustable device that allows players to hit a stationary ball.

Bunt: An intentionally soft hit. (*Note:* There is no bunting in tee ball.) See also *playing line*.

Catcher: The player positioned behind *home plate*. Primarily responsible for tagging incoming runners.

Coach-pitch: A game format for more experienced players where the coach throws the ball to the batter. No tee is used unless a player is unable to hit the pitched ball.

Crow-hop: A step-together-step foot action used to provide more throwing momentum after fielding a ball.

Dead ball: A ball no longer in play, for instance, if it is not hit past the *playing line*.

Dead ball zone: The area of the infield between *home plate* and the *playing line*.

Diamond: The tee ball field of play; technically, the infield.

Double: A two-base hit.

Double play: A single defensive play following a hit ball that results in two *outs*.

Error: A misplay by a defensive player.

Fair ball: A batted ball that lands in or goes over *fair territory*.

Fair territory: The playing field between and including the foul lines.

Fielder's choice: A defensive play in which a fielder tries to throw out a *base runner* instead of the *batter*.

First-base player: The infielder positioned near the first-base bag.

Fly ball: A ball hit high in the air to the outfield.

Fly out: A ball caught before it touches the ground.

Follow-through: The part of the throwing motion that occurs after the ball is released, or the part of the swing that occurs after the bat has gone through the contact area.

Force-out: An out made when a runner is required to advance to another base and the fielder with the ball tags the runner or touches the base before the runner arrives.

Foul ball: A ball hit into *foul territory*.

Foul poles: Two markers set at the end of each foul line, usually at an outfield wall, that determine if the ball is fair or foul. A ball that hits a pole is fair.

Foul territory: All area outside the foul lines.

Fungo: A ball hit for fielding practice. The coach tosses a ball into the air and hits it to the fielders.

Grand slam: A *home run* hit with the bases loaded.

Ground ball: A batted ball that rolls or bounces along the ground.

Grounder: See *ground ball*.

Ground out: An *out* made by one or more defensive players on a *ground ball*.

Hit: See *base hit*.

Home plate: A five-sided slab where the batter stands. Also the base that is stepped on or touched by a runner to score (in a game where scores are kept).

Home run: A four-base hit, or a fair *fly ball* that carries over an outfield fence or marked boundary. (*Note:* In tee ball, most home runs are made when the batter can safely circle the bases before the defensive team can secure the ball and make an out.)

Infielder: A defensive player positioned within or near the *diamond* formed by the four *bases*.

Infield fly rule: A fair *fly ball* caught by an *infielder* when two or more offensive players are on base. The batter is automatically out. (*Note:* This only applies when there are two outs in a game where outs are kept.)

Inning: A division of the game (actually, two half innings) when both teams bat and play in the field.

Line drive: A hard hit ball that travels in a straight line.

Mitt: A glove with no fingers, except for the thumb. Used by first-base players and catchers.

On deck: The position of the next offensive player to bat.

Out: A play when a batter or runner cannot safely reach a base.

Outfielder: A defensive player positioned in *fair territory* well beyond the infield.

Pitcher: The defensive player positioned in the pitcher's circle or near where a pitcher would stand. Also the person (often a coach) who delivers pitches to the batters in the coach-pitch game format.

Pitcher's circle: The area where the defensive player acting as pitcher or a coach-pitcher is positioned.

Playing line: A real or imaginary line between first and third base or an arc extending out from *home plate*.

Pop fly: A *fly ball* hit high and in the air over the infield or nearby outfield.

Pop-up: See *pop fly*.

Pre-tee ball: An introductory training game for very young participants. Field measurements, team size, and playing time are modified.

Relay: A play where an outfielder throws the ball to another defensive player who then throws the ball to a teammate covering a base.

Run: In games where scores are kept, a point awarded to an offensive team when a player has safely touched all four bases.

Runner: An offensive player moving toward, returning to, or standing on a base.

Safe: When an offensive player gets to a base before being thrown out or *tagged out*.

Safety helmet: Helmets made of high-impact plastic are required for the batter, the on-deck batter, all base runners, the catcher, and the first- and third-base coaches.

Second-base player: The infielder positioned near the second-base bag in the first-base side of the infield.

Shortstop: The infielder positioned between second and third base but closer to second base.

Single: A one-base hit.

Slide: A baserunning technique in which a runner tries to avoid being tagged by sliding on the ground toward the base.

Stealing: The act of advancing to the next base after the pitcher releases the ball. (*Note:* There is no stealing in tee ball.)

Strike: A pitch when the batter swings and misses or hits the ball into foul territory. (*Note:* There are no strikes in tee ball.)

Tag out: The act of a fielder tagging a batter or base runner. The fielder can step on a base before the offensive player arrives there or touch the runner with the ball.

Tag up: The act of a base runner returning to touch a base after a fly ball is caught. The runner may then try to advance to the next base.

Tee ball: A softer and safer version (usually with a sponge rubber center) of a standard baseball.

Third-base player: The infielder positioned near the third-base bag.

Triple: A three-base hit.

Umpire: The ruling official in a tee ball game.

Walk: See *base on balls*.

Resources

Associations and Organizations

Babe Ruth League, Inc.
1770 Brunswick Pike
Trenton NJ 08638
609-695-1434
www.baberuthleague.org
Tee ball is now played within the Cal Ripken Division of this outstanding organization committed to the betterment of youth and producing skilled players. Local leagues are independent and operate under guidelines provided by the Babe Ruth International Board.

Boys & Girls Clubs of America
1230 West Peachtree St. NW
Atlanta GA 30309
404-815-5700
www.bgca.org
Tee ball is offered by many local Boys & Girls Clubs as part of their sports, fitness, and recreation program. The emphasis is on teamwork, skill development, and the enjoyment of a group activity.

Dixie Youth Baseball
P.O. Box 877
Marshall TX 75671
903-927-2255
Fax: 903-927-1846
E-mail: dyb@dixie.org
www.dixieyb.org
The Dixie philosophy is to emphasize local autonomy in the belief that parents and organizers in a community know what is best for them and their children. The A Division offers tee ball for players age 6 and under; the AA Division offers coach-pitch for players age 8 and under. Each state organization adopts its own playing rules for both divisions.

Dizzy Dean Baseball
National Headquarters
224 Sandy Hwy. 51
Hernando MI 38362
662-429-4365
www.dbb.org
The T-Ball division of Dizzy Dean Baseball has been organized as a program open to 5- and 6-year-olds, regardless of gender, color, religion, or race. The Farm League has coach-pitch (and player pitch) for players up to 8 years old. Leagues are franchised within communities, or by smaller towns joining together to form a league.

Little League Baseball, Inc.
P.O. Box 3485
Williamsport PA 17701
570-326-1921
www.littleleague.org
Little League Tee Ball is a training process by which 5- to 8-year-olds can learn, develop, and practice fundamental skills at an early age and receive maximum enjoyment from the experience. The rules suggested are recommendations from Little League Headquarters and may be adjusted appropriately to meet individual program needs. Little League has been instrumental in the growth of organized tee ball play and administers a quality

program throughout the country and internationally.

Little League Canada
235 Dale Ave.
Ottawa ON K1G 0H6
CANADA
613-731-3301
Fax: 613-731-2829
E-mail: canada@littleleague.org
www.littleleague.ca
The Canadian program operates under the same basic rules and philosophy as the U.S. program. Youngsters are offered a place where they can learn fundamental skills and have fun at an early age.

Major League Baseball (MLB)
245 Park Ave.
New York NY 10167
212-931-7500
www.mlb.com
The Office of the Commissioner and each MLB team supports youth baseball in many ways. Tee ball groups benefit from various activities and events (such as participation at the MLB FanFest clinics and exhibition games and opportunities to attend MLB games) and the interest of the MLB in the growth of the sport which is, in effect, the gateway to baseball. RBI, the Reviving Baseball in Inner Cities program, focuses on an important part of youth development.

National Alliance for Youth Sports (NAYS)
2050 Vista Pkwy.
West Palm Beach FL 33411
800-729-2057; 800-688-KIDS
  (800-688-5437); 561-684-1141

Fax: 561-684-2546
E-mail: nays@nays.org
www.nays.org
NAYS provides programs that train volunteers who administer and coach in organized youth sports. Its Web site offers information on various educational programs, such as the National Youth Sports Coaches Association, which has educational material for volunteer coaches in organized out of school sports.

National Association of Police Athletic Leagues
618 U.S. Hwy. 1, Suite 201
North Palm Beach FL 33408-4609
561-844-1823
Fax: 561-863-6120
E-mail: copnkid@nationalpal.org
www.nationalpal.org
Tee ball is offered by individual PAL chapters. Check locally for an available program and facility.

National Council of Youth Sports (NCYS)
7185 SE Seagate Lane
Stuart FL 34997
772-781-1452
Fax: 772-781-7298
www.ncys.org
A multisport nonprofit corporation established to strengthen the performance of youth sport administrators through education and to advocate the values and preserve the integrity of organized youth sports. Tee ball is represented by the membership of senior executives of various organizations that offer and support the game.

National Recreation and Park Association (NRPA)
22377 Belmont Ridge Rd.
Ashburn VA 20148-4501
703-858-0784
Fax: 703-858-0794
E-mail: info@nrpa.org
www.nrpa.org
The NRPA mission includes advancing parks and recreation to "enhance the quality of life for all people." Consequently, tee ball is widely played on municipal facilities either as part of Parks and Recreation programs or as physical locations for various community leagues.

North American Youth Sports Institute (NAYSI)
4985 Oak Garden Dr.
Kernersville NC 27284-9520
800-767-4916; 336-784-4926
Fax: 336-784-5546
www.naysi.com
NAYSI provides a range of sports-oriented information, technical support, and instructional training for parents, coaches, community youth work professionals, and groups involved in recreational and fitness activities.

PONY Baseball and Softball, Inc.
International Headquarters
P.O. Box 225
Washington PA 15301
724-225-1060
Fax: 724-225-9852
www.pony.org.
PONY, an acronym for Protect Our Nation's Youth, is dedicated to providing baseball and softball experiences that will help young people grow into healthier and happier

adults. Tee ball is generally played in the Shetland League (ages 5 and 6) and sometimes, in the Pinto League (ages 7 and 8). The organization has an excellent Web site.

Sporting Goods Manufacturers Association (SGMA)
200 Castlewood Dr.
North Palm Beach FL 33408-5695
561-842-4100
www.sgma.com
SGMA is the global business trade association of manufacturers and marketers of sports apparel, athletic footwear, sporting goods equipment, and related recreational merchandise. It stages a major trade show and generates important market research and relevant communications. SGMA members provide most of the products used by tee ball leagues and is an excellent source of information.

T•BALL USA Academy, Inc.
21 3rd Ave.
Bay Shore NY 11706
631-665-CAMP (631-665-2267)
Fax: 631-665-9231
The academy provides camps and clinics and other programs, products, and activities related to early-age tee ball instruction.

T•BALL USA Association, Inc.
2499 Main St.
Stratford CT 06615
203-381-1449
Fax: 203-381-1440
E-mail: teeballusa@aol.com
www.teeballusa.org
The national nonprofit organization dedicated to the development of

the game. It assists all tee ball groups to maximize the effectiveness of their programs and to provide specific benefits that enhance participation by all concerned.

USA Baseball
Hi Corbett Field
3400 East Camino Campestre
Tucson AZ 85716
520-327-9700
Fax: 520-327-9231
E-mail: usabaseball@aol.com
www.usabaseball.com
USA Baseball, the national governing body for the sport, is responsible for promoting and developing the game on the grassroots level nationally and internationally. It is a resource center for its various membership groups, which include organizations that offer tee ball programs.

YMCA of the USA
101 North Wacker Dr.
Chicago IL 60606
312-977-0031
www.ymca.net
The YMCA is one of the most active providers of quality tee ball activity. Their program is based on skill training, participation, teamwork, fair play, fitness, family involvement, volunteers, and fun.

Publications and Electronic Newsletters

Junior Baseball
P.O. Box 9099
Canoga Park CA 91309
818-710-1234
Fax: 818-710-1877

www.juniorbaseball.com
"America's Youth Baseball Magazine" is the national publication dedicated to providing expert information to players, their parents, coaches, and associated organizations, regardless of league, park, or school affiliation. It features a regular tee ball column (the Rookie Club) for ages 5 to 8.

Youth Sports Newsletter
www.youth-sports.com
A free e-mail newsletter for parents, coaches, and children covering a broad range of topics; such as nutrition, fitness, skill development, and related matters. Tee ball instructional material is featured. It is published on or about the 15th of every month, and previous issues are archived for reading, downloading, and printing.

Suppliers

American Baseball Cap Company
P.O. Box 878
Chadds Ford PA 19317
484-840-1925
Fax: 484-840-1927
E-mail: abchelmets.com
www.abchelmets.com
The originators of the batting (safety) helmet, the American Baseball Cap Company is the official helmet supplier to Major League Baseball, USA Baseball, and Minor League Baseball.

The Little Tikes Company
2180 Barlow Rd.
Hudson OH 44236
800-231-0183

www.littletikes.com
Little Tikes manufactures and markets high-quality, innovative children's products that are durable, imaginative, and fun, like the TotSports T-Ball Set shown on page 110. Go to their Web site to find local retailers of their products.

Regent Sports Company
45 Ranick Rd.
Hauppauge NY 11788
631-234-2800; 800-645-5190
E-mail: custserv@regent-halex.com

www.regent-halex.com
Regent Sports is a leading supplier of sporting goods equipment, including affordable quality tee ball products for family and league use.

Sowell Sports Photography
313 West 9½ Mile Rd.
Pensacola FL 32534
313-969-1831
E-mail: sports@spydee.net
www.genessports.com
Specializes in sports action and team picture photography.

Index

Acknowledgments

I want to thank each of the individuals who contributed the sidebar comments, drills, tips, and related material that enhance my text. They are identified throughout the book. Special appreciation is also extended to all who have supported our association and the game of tee ball.

Additional recognition is due to Chuck Ashman, Carol Banning, Al Bender, Anna Bridgman, Tony Burns, Dick Case, Anthony Cosenza, Mike Fagundes, Carl Ferraro, Dick Jones, Kelly Hayward, Pam Marshall, Mike May, Edward Palmer, Amber Rae, Marc Steir, and my home team— Belinda Broido, Andy Kenoe, and Amy and Randy Rabenhorst. The finished book reflects the talents of Margaret Cook, Jon Eaton, and Molly Mulhern, and the photographic skill of Gene Sowell.

The author, throwing out the first ball in a ceremony before a recent game in Arlington, Texas, between the Texas Rangers and the Chicago White Sox. Linda Kaye

About the Author

H. W. "Bing" Broido is the cofounder and president of the T•BALL USA Association, the nonprofit organization that administers T•BALL USA and T•BALL WORLD. He is the author of *The Official T•BALL USA Family Guide to Tee Ball*, and *The Book of Rules*, an authoritative guide to the official rules and playing procedures of fifty sports. Prior to assuming leadership of T•BALL USA, he was president of a consumer products marketing firm. He developed merchandise programs under the sponsorship of many international, government, and private sector organizations and celebrities in such areas as art, entertainment, home furnishings, fashion, sports, and fitness. A graduate of Dartmouth College, he is a lifelong sports enthusiast and a member of the National Council of Youth Sports.